Housewife Blues

~

dispatches from the garden of broken things

DINA STANDER

Published by Human Error Publishing
www.humanerrorpublishing.com
paul@humanerrorpublishing.com

ISBN: 978-1-948521-02-4

Front Cover Photo: Dina Stander
Back Cover Photo: Dina Stander

for Betsy
~
(dnpt)

Paul Bobrowitz ~ metal art in Wisconsin

About the photos in this book...

Why are they here? Well may you wonder.

Except for three, I took the photos here myself.
The portrait of my mother and her sister was taken by my
mother's partner at my wedding, and I found the sardines on
Unsplash. The photo of the frog was taken by my husband.
The flowers are genuine blossoms from the garden of broken
things. The meditating dog lives there too. There are a number of found object collage assemblages tucked away here
that are part of an ongoing art project (one blessing of getting older is that you get to see the longer trajectory of your
work). And you'll also encounter the specific sort of absurd
juxtapositions I stumble upon wandering about the world
which deeply appeal to my sense of humor. Like a cafe sign, a
random pile of spoons, or Burger Bob and the Buddha. Some
of the photos offer the respite of beauty. Some are placed to
underline a certain tension. I added the photos as a nod to
the unspoken, a respectful tip o' my cap to the echoes between the lines. And another way to connect. Thank you for
your time and consideration.

Table of Contents

First Words

Welcome to the garden of broken things. It is a real place, a haphazard collection of plants and found objects, stones, statues, odd rusting implements, stumps, and seashells left where bees can find water. A good place to be a toad. A garden where all the favorite plates and mugs my children accidentally dropped could find new ways to be favorites. A place where a thing does not have to be whole to be of good use by contributing beauty to life. The cast iron pan that split is there. And the remains of my grandmother's fancy bowl.

For a spine-injured gardener who bends gingerly and can't quite pull weeds, the garden of broken things is a sanctuary filled with ordinary pleasures, an investment in beauty. It is the place where I found respite from the challenges I faced being a disabled mother raising a neurodiverse family in a world built for able bodied and neuro-typical people. My three children are grown now but the garden's idiosyncrasies continue to nourish my spirit.

I tried not to get bogged down in finding a sensible order for the essays in this book. They are written over a span of 20 years; some have been previously published, some have been read from stages at festivals and open mics. There is a youtube video of Hung Like a Horse, a piece that was specifi -

cally written to be read aloud. This is a book I hope you will open at random to see what rises to the top.

I am sending this manuscript off to my publisher in the last days of 2020. Can you see I feel concerned? I know there is a line being drawn across the arc of my time: writing before 2020 and writing from within the covidiverse. As usual, we are where we are. Housewife Blues is a collection of pre-covidiverse thought experiments. So much of what takes place in our lives is lost between the lines.

What I have learned recently is that if I wait until I get it 'right' then nothing much happens at all. So here with all their imperfections I offer a collection of essays and writing that has been cheerfully fermenting for some time. It's ready for some traveling shoes. As we say in our house, thank you to meet you. Wishing you safe travels and the blessing of enough. ~ ds

Turning Soil

My friend Bea died from cancer on a painfully sweet May morning, the day before Mother's Day. My calendar said full moon and I smiled in spite of the ache. How like her to go when the tides are pulling us towards light; a morning full of new leaves, bird song, and a slow rain.

I have a favorite technicolor memory of Bea from another May morning. Typically audacious, she wore white in her garden - a floppy hat, long sleeves, pants tucked into socks. Her muscled arms thrusting a spade deep, she looked like a vital Spring goddess turning soil, trees in flower and the sun shining a glory around her body. Her absolute desire to get dirty was so delicious that I drove by waving madly out the window. She had survived the winter of her first bout with cancer.

Adult friendships between women busy raising children is whole-cloth woven from interrupted conversations sewn together with the thread of goodwill over a continuum of years. We were coming to some especially interesting patterns in the cloth when death interrupted my conversation with Bea. Once, while I rubbed her hands warm during a hospital visit, relating tribulations with my kids, she gently admonished me to "just go home and love them up, hold them closer." Following this advice is not always easy but it is usually what works best. It was a simple lesson in redemption, a gift from a mother who loved fiercely and wanted so much to stay.

Another time I visited after a bad night. The nurses had moved her next to a window and we sat looking out together. Everything was bare, flat hospital rooftops and April's naked branches. Early Spring is a hard time for hope in New England because winter holds on tight. I read to her for a while, then massaged her feet in their wildly colored socks. In a hospital johnny, hooked up to IV fluids and pallor gray from chemotherapy, socks were how Bea reminded us of her soul. And of our own.

Bea was the kind of friend who reflects back for you the parts of yourself you don't necessarily appreciate enough or want to let show (or have learned to hide). She saw me in a way that allowed for how intense I can be. She reminded me once that I couldn't help being this way, it was all part of the package. Her understanding gave me courage in a critical moment to go on being myself. It is this courage, which I still associate with her colorful socks, that I carry forward.

I asked Bea once why she thought we incarnate, souls taking bodies to play out the inevitably painful human drama. She replied that it must be because living is such an interesting torrent of experience: to feel, taste, touch, smell, hear, see, learn, make and create, perchance to love. From the loneliness and sterility of a dying person's hospital bed this insight gifted me with seeds I plant, season after season, while turning the soil of my inner garden; the one I tend to keep from feeling broken. It is Mother's Day again, and again I am blessed by the memory of my friend's fierce loving, reminded to sense everything, and especially to give thanks for the feel of my kids arms around me, and mine around them.

How I Dance: Disability & Mothering

Walk a mile in any shoes

Yesterday, as I rested at the half way point in my daily mile, down and up the road again, I sat on a boulder where the stream crosses under the road. I watched the water and reflected on the word 'disability'.

This word has come to be a boundary in my life. There is before, when I believed I could always get better from 'episodes' of back pain: there is after, episodes becoming instead the way life is.

These days I can walk a mile and a bit more if I rest in the middle and don't mind the neuropathic oddity of not quite being connected to my legs in the last stretch towards home. In recent years I have used both a walker and an electric scooter to cover the same territory.

Seasons

There are days, even weeks, when being disabled seems like a steady accumulation of discomfort and frustration. Through the six months winter lingers in New England my body devises new ways to work less well; there are more things I can almost-but-not-quite do because they are at the edge of my ability, or because they are on the other side of an icy street.

There are bad days when I want to complain, at length but not bitterly; in a manner that will somehow absolve me of the sin of complaint. Even more, free me of the need for complaint. I want the liberty to moan about pain and the list of things I cannot or should not do. When sensation in my legs or fingers begins to fade away I want to bellow at them to come back and behave.

I desire most of all a season of neutrality, a time when I am not concerned with good and bad days, when a day can be just a day.

Optimism

My optimism is the same as a tree bud's in the deep of winter. My optimism is a utilitarian brown, it protects tirelessly yet can drop away in the wind, and will grow in new when I need it again. It hangs out there at the tips of things, although vulnerable itself, and wraps around my tender anticipations for spring and relief.

Bitterness

Bitterness is the off-flavor note in my emotional soup. I try to disguise it with a salt tongue because the savory bite is distracting and other people seem more comfortable with salt, more accommodating of it's grains.

Bitter rolls in on a wave the first time the snow gets deep enough and my children go out with sleds to fly down the hillside, screaming at the top of their lungs. I sit at the window wanting so badly to be out there with them that my breath comes ragged and tears burn across my cheeks because with my whole being I can remember going so fast, feeling so cold, so alive. I want to believe that life can be this much fun, still.

Bitterness strikes like a whip, leaves a cracking hot streak across the air between me and whoever touched the nerve. No matter how inadvertently. No matter how often I've wanted to pluck words back and burn them in the heat of my remorse. The backlash stings my sinuses and psyche. I fumble for ways to make amends, tucking the grief away again.

Things I Hate About Chronic Pain

I hate the way chronic pain makes a narcissist out of an otherwise reasonable and caring person. I hate how much I have to try not to talk about myself because I've become so needy for someone to care about how I feel living in my body, to understand how much work it can be to get through a day.

Pain comes with me wherever I go. On average days I can ignore it all and float on top somehow. On bad days I'm sometimes able to set the pain itself on another channel which I don't have to watch. But elsewhere in my brain the pain is noted and, although my attention is purposely turned away, synapses are sparking an array of simultaneous responses and the whole dancing organism that embodies me is so busy coping that by 4:30 in the afternoon, just when my family needs dinner started, I realize I have no energy left.

Floating on Memory and Dreams

Once spring sets in with warmer weather and the fear of ice passes, the mile I am able to walk is a tremendous gift. I live on a dirt road in a forest where walking is a chance to encounter life: birds chatter, barred owls hoot from one hemlock grove to another; a porcupine perched on a high branch scolds from it's safe distance. I sometimes find small bones a raptor has left on a stump or spy a lady slipper, exotic and pink by the roadside, it's beauty so delicate that I tremble. I imagine opening the memory centers in my brain and absorbing images, smells, sounds, textures, patterns of light and root; taking it on faith that I'll be able to replay it all when my body no longer allows me the first hand experience of a walk in the woods.

I sometimes dream I live in a body at ease in itself. In one dream I run like a child through a field of tall grass, waking just as I am about to fall; heart pounding, still tasting sun and green. I am glad for the brain's ability to store experience in these technicolor displays. I lay in bed immersed in this wild freedom that abides in me and try with all my might to relay it towards whichever bundles of tissue and nerve sustain my capacity for wholeness.

Transcendence

I stand on my own, even if it's not my own two feet. I don't want my accomplishments and failures to be measured in light of disability. Yet disability has made boundaries in my life and sharpened my personality; it seeks outlet through creativity and shadows my closest relationships. As I grow more intimate with the reality of being a disabled person it becomes clear that disability is shaping how I define myself in my family and in the world.

Our paraplegic neighbor who plows his own driveway, my cousin with severe cerebral palsy who is a college graduate and mother, the two friends who have rheumatoid arthritis, and the 98 year old active senior-center volunteer I met who is so frustrated by recent ocular degeneration . . . none of these people overcome their disabilities. Overcoming implies an end somehow, a cessation of the disabling condition and the personal grief it causes. We are only ordinary human beings, unlikely candidates for miracle cures.

Instead of overcoming, I seek to expand what I can do. Most of my attempts are inconsequential outside the banal sphere of my day to day life. I make unremarkable efforts to gerrymander skills, balance limitations, and adapt environments to accommodate my abilities. Sometimes I achieve this with a grace bordering on the miraculous, but not any more often than able-bodied people find grace.

Disability is something I transcend on a daily basis, every time I have to apologize for snapping at my children when Mrs. Grump inhabits my mind. There is an inner physics to

transcendence, rooted in the capacity to give oneself a clean slate every morning. It takes practice.

A Dance of Possibility

Hope, I find, provides insufficient energy for living and coping with an aging body and chronic pain. Am I to hope for a cure or some newfangled surgical solution? For better pain meds with fewer side effects? For a solar-electric four wheel drive titanium scooter with enough ground clearance and juice that I could safely take myself off-road? I will be hoping for a long, long time. Instead I dance with what is possible, embracing what is and making my awkward peace with reality. To transcend being sad that I cannot sled with my children in the first good snow of winter, I sit with myself and imagine I am on the sled. That I can feel where the snow has wedged deep in my boots, making my ankles cold. That I am holding on and flying as fast as the wind, red-cheeked and free. That I cannot quite steer but miss the tree anyway and make the bump that lifts me airborne for those few seconds. That when I finally come to a stop I am laughing so hard it makes me need to pee.

When I am done with all the breathless exhilaration in my own mind, I go to the kitchen and make us all hot chocolate. I will take it out to them in the snow. Because this is what is possible and it is good.

I Have a Few Things to Say

The world is coming apart at the seams.

I don't know most days how to cope with the innermost distress I feel about Spring coming six weeks early and not being able to afford to send my kids to college and all of the faltering economies. Magnolias are blooming in March in New England and tornadoes cut a ninety five mile swath through Kentucky and Tennessee. It's all connected, and I haven't even mentioned the bad stuff yet.

I am stealing a moment from an otherwise busy day to tell you, I can't pretend it's not happening. The oil spill in the Gulf of Mexico, meltdown at Fukushima; disasters that keep on giving. I am dismayed that human beings have crapped the bed this way. Why now, why in my lifetime? I thought I incarnated to dance and play, not to watch the planet spin into disarray.

I want to acknowledge us all for the every day hero's journey we somehow pull off. I am so amazed that we all have the chutzpah to roll out of bed each morning and put our feet on the floor and begin another day in the face of such over-whelming evidence that everything is all fucked up.

Yet each day begins anew, humanity teetering on the brink of possibility and disaster, my heart beating the rhythm of my life in a steady miracle of hope. "Hope is the thing with feathers..." (with a tip o' the pen to Emily Dickinson) and while mine perches it is perhaps molting a little. I can see the disharmony is caused by the weather and not my imagina-tion, the over-neath and underneath all swirling together, the somewhat foreboding sense that calamitous events beyond our control could be just around the bend...

Yet, we begin each day with a breath, a stretch, we rub the sleep from the corners of our eyes, we pee and fart and scratch. We pull our pants on one leg at a time. I have decided that this is the most courageous and endearing act of being human, putting on our pants. Keeping it simple, you see. Life is good.

Reaching around in the dark a while back I ran into that old hippie meme, Be Here Now. Lately I find that having the capacity to reset my awareness to here and now is truly helpful. The Mountain of Things I Cannot Fix has become insurmountable and I cannot swim across the Sea of Debt lapping at the shores of my personal equanimity. So I take a breath, I look around, there is always beauty staring me in the face, grass and dandelions growing up between cracks in the asphalt. There is always a reason to attend to the present, to look at what is unfolding in this moment I have stolen for us, there is only now, and now, and now.

And everything is still terrible. And everything is plain wonderful. We are well enough. And I take a breath. Gain perspective. Here we are sailing on an arm of the Milky Way, hurtling through the Universe on this little Earth. What are three things I know are true right now:

1. We are made of the same atoms originating from the same moment in time as all the other star stuff is made of. All One Universe.

2. I am blessed because today I could put my pants on without falling on my face.

3. Fear cannot stop me from loving.

If I let myself consider what is actually going on, our world is scaring the shit out of me most of the time. Still, I roll out of bed in the morning and pull my pants on one leg at a time. Still, when I step out my front door I greet the day and give thanks for my continued existence.

Still, on the way home later I slide open the window of my car and stop the engine so that I can listen to the peeper frogs singing into the night and let their music sail right through me, realigning the polar charges of every cell in my body and pointing me towards ALIVE, so that the remedy for my distress over everything is here, where it is always now, with the frogs and the night and the wind sighing through the pines. And here on the page with you, where we are indulging in a stolen moment to engage in the vulnerable foolishness of being human.

This moment is the gift of existing, a little reality blip to share as we hurtle willy nilly through space and time and the complications of our quaint human dramas. In this moment, because we have set it aside to say we are here, now, where our hearts beat together in syncopation with every other heart, and as the moment unfolds itself it is as if the time stream opens in a delicate 'Oh' of surprise and we get a glimpse of the crack in everything and I remember that Leonard Cohen riff about how important the crack in everything is, because "that's how the light gets in."

That's what I'm thinking about, with this stolen moment sitting on my shoulder, saying to me, "Crack it open fool!" I am, just as I am, cracked in such a way that I hope lets the light in; the light from the beginning of time, the breath of life, the here and now. This place where all the divine fools, having perched long enough to have their resilience restored, bow and wink to one another, then spin around and begin again.

Even though the world is coming apart at the seams.

Safe

I ran in to a Mom-acquaintance in the supermarket the other morning. A woman whose husband died last year, leaving her with an infant son and two older boys to raise on her own. 'Mom-acquaintance' is my word for the women I know only because our children go to the same school; we think of each other as so-and-so's mom and struggle to locate first names in challenged internal memory banks. Her eldest son and my eldest daughter were in pre-school together. Her name is June, and I don't ever forget because I too am a mother of three, and the very idea of losing my husband paralyzes me with dread. I can see in June's eyes that she has been to the edge and slipped over. And that she has survived. There is some certain strength I see in her, tempered by deep sadness. It makes me shudder to think of it being necessary to become so strong.

I say all this because this afternoon I returned home from the grocery store, up a steep and icy single lane dirt road, praying no one was coming down the other way. My youngest girl fell asleep in her car seat with her head cranked to one side in toddler oblivion. I made it up the last gauntlet hill without sliding into the ditch and was distracted with strategies of how to get the groceries out of the car without waking the toddler. Half up my drive way I noticed my husband's car parked in its usual spot, but it should have been 79 miles east of here in the parking lot at his office. I left my car running to keep the kid warm, shoes skidding across the treacherous walkway, up the steps, into the house. I completely forgot the groceries.

I heard my husband move from his chair in the office as I came through the door. He came into the hallway smiling in a way I have learned to recognize as more nervous than happy. Just as I noticed the red scrape in the middle of his forehead he said in his most reassuring voice, "First you should know that I am really ok. Really. But my car is totaled."

I am married to a man who commutes an hour and fifteen minutes each way to work. He loves his work and we love where we live and neither of us wants to move. This morning I left to take the kids to school knowing the roads would be slippery. I said to him, "I want you back safe and whole, please drive carefully." I often say this to him and he generally smiles back at me before rolling his eyes towards the ceiling in an of-course-I-will sigh; feeling loved and cared for, knowing that he matters a lot to me. Now I am thinking I should have mentioned that I wanted the car back safe and sound as well.

As I write I am listening to my husband at his desk talking to our youngest daughter. He is trying to work and she is on his lap flirting with all her might (and she is a mighty flirt) to keep him in her thrall. I can tell from his patient tone, from the way he caresses her head, that he is feeling the delicious weight of all the precious moments our children bring us. Life is so tenuous. I keep wanting to touch him, to lay my hands on his skin where I can feel he is warm and alive. The sound of his voice helps my own heart to beat in it's accustomed steady rhythm.

After he reassured me again that he was unhurt, I settled the toddler into her nap. Then I dragged my husband to our bed so that I could lay with him under the covers with all our clothes still on, and convince myself that he was not some corporeal apparition come to say his goodbyes as kindly as possible. My relief felt too close to grief and he wanted to return to his desk much sooner than I was ready to let go my grip on his body. I made him talk to me. I closed my eyes and lay my head on his chest listening to his internal music: heart, breath, and voice. A symphony of comfort and security.

Loving is filled with the risks of pain and loss, I accepted this truth when I accepted this person as my life partner. Losing him wouldn't be the end of me, though I'd be undone for a time. This afternoon I could see how easily I'd unravel--at least until my children needed me to tie up my lose ends and make a nest for their own hungry grief. I don't like to be reminded of the mortality of people I love. I like to think that we will just keep growing older and loving more and having small (and grand) adventures. "No such luck," whispers Death, though not unkindly.

Which leads me back around to my Mom-acquaintance, June. She said in the grocery store, when I asked how she was getting along, that a glass of wine at ten o'clock at night makes all the difference. I'm not fond of close calls or of being reminded of how fragile our hold is on the security of a two-parent family. It's only two in the afternoon now, but that glass of wine is looking wonderfully attractive. I lift my glass to June. And then I lift it again to whichever guardian angel (or fickle finger of fate) brought my husband home again today. L'chaim, to life.

Tree Season

By the Sunday after Thanksgiving we've usually run out of A-list leftovers, so I head to town for groceries and immediately notice: the holiday tree season has begun.

Wherever I go I see conifers strapped to the tops of cars, destined for lights and heirloom finery. All will end up desiccated, stripped and discarded sometime in January. Clearly I have mixed feelings about Christmas trees. I'm a secular Jew married to a person who has happy cultural, rather than religious, ties to Christmas. My mother does not visit in December in order to avoid uncomfortable feelings about a tree in my house. But I can't avoid how uncomfortable it makes me, the Rabbi's granddaughter, ever aware that assimilation is a slippery slope.

It was a moot point until our eldest child was two and a half and attended a family daycare where Christmas was Fun. The inevitable question was popped on the drive home, "Mommy, where is OUR qwitmas twee?"

"You should ask Daddy about that," I side-stepped. She did, as soon as he got home.

"Daddy, where is OUR qwitmas twee?" Stand back Cindy-Lou Who – my daughter now embodied the innocence of Christmas. I expected Daddy to explain that we don't need trees to make holidays special, but daddies are notorious suckers for little girls. Instead he replied, "Let's go get one."

Huh? "Wait a minute," I sputtered, "a Christmas tree? We're Jewish!" It always catches me by surprise to be reminded my marriage bridges cultural boundaries. Nine years we'd lived together and never discussed having a tree.

"I understand your reservations but I'm not Jewish," my husband replied, "I like having a tree and it will be fun, let's get one." It was simple...for him. Sharing the tree tradition was about cultural continuity. My daughter loves the smell of cooking tsimmes, she could love the scent of balsam too. I had no good reason to say no. Thus began the annual love-hate thing I have going with Christmas trees.

Over the ensuing years, as our family has grown, we've compromised. We CAN decorate a tree. But. There are a list of no's. No tinsel. No angels, no Santas! No crosses or leaping lords, and no baby gods. Nothing Jewish! The tree can have anything from nature; pinecones, nests, shells, butterfly wings, favorite rocks, even bones. We add animal ornaments and hang pretty postcards. Lights are in, but not blinking ones. Fairies and mythical creatures are ok, within reason: Godzilla yes (classic), Shrek no (commercial), there is an ancient goddess or two and my favorite ornament, a small picture of John Lennon (a tip of my Holiday cap to the world I can imagine).

What fits on, of course, brings up size of tree. I cannot be trusted to choose a tree: I'm a 'Charlie Brown." I pick trees that are gimpy, sparse or otherwise challenged; if it's small, bent, or has a bare patch I'll claim it until one of my children drags me aside, "Mom, NOT that tree, it's just wrong, let's look over here." I am directed to a row of full, handsome trees, which I reject. My husband watches and smiles.

"Why can't we just get this one, the underdog tree?" I ask, holding up a pathetic specimen. "It's worthy, it needs a home."

"Mom," grumbles the 8 year old, "that branch was cut from the bottom of a bigger tree, give us a break."

"Can't this be the year we don't have a tree?" I stage whisper, so that legitimate tree hunters won't hear me. I'm an imposter, I don't know from Christmas trees.

"Mom, it's just a tree, besides they only sell Solstice trees here," gentles my eldest. She's been through this before:

mama pleads on behalf of the scrawniest tree, balks at having any tree, and is then encouraged to embrace non-Christian tree traditions.

Eventually we find the right tree for our family, not tall or bushy, and it only needs three good sides to look content in the corner. I pay, we tie it to the roof. Oddly, I never feel more obviously Jewish than when I've strapped a tree to the car. I'm faking it, I've stolen the Christian's tree. I get out of town fast.

I wonder some about the stories my children will tell about their meshugannah mama, but I have a suspicion they'll also be drawn to champion underdog trees. There's a lot to be said for cultural continuity in a melting-pot family, however we arrive at it.

Happy To Be Here

Near the wide bottom step to the porch of my cousin's cabin on a back road in Indiana, nestled in the tall grass that the mower misses, sits a dented metal coffee pot. Chipped paint shows it's been more than one color, stood humbly on more than one stove and by more than one doorstep. I noticed the coffee pot right off when I arrived, though it was hiding and I hadn't visited here before.

Sometimes an object feels like a relative; I have felt related to more than one old dented metal coffee pot. I didn't give it much thought until my mother arrived a few days later. I came outside the cabin and found her bent over, inspecting something at the bottom of the steps. Her old-lady hands parted the grass around the pot. She looked up at me, squinting in the morning sun, mischief in her smile.

"That's my mother's coffee pot but how did it get here?"

"Maybe it just looks like your mother's coffee pot," I answered.

"Well, it wasn't green or red in Brooklyn," she said, picking at the chipping paint, evidence of some gardener's changing mood. The undercoat, also chipping, was white enamel.

"That's Mother's coffee pot," chirped my aunt, clinging to the rail as she descended the porch steps, "she gave it to me."
"See," said my mom, "I'd know it anywhere."

"I had it in Cincinnati, how did it get here? Katey, I think I want that pot back, put it in my car," she directs her daughter, monarch to minion: one bird-thin hand sweeping a regal indication from pot to car, the other hand clinging to the rail.

My cousin and mother exchange a glance, knowing the coffee pot will be forgotten in moments. Still, both look wounded; my mother because it was given to her sister and not to her self, my cousin by the resonant power of her own mother's giving and taking away, a blade wielded now out of habit but no less sharp.

Cousin takes aunt by arm and I am left sitting beside my mother on the sun-warmed wooden step, listening to birds and the wide creek winding through the tall grass in the pasture across the road. Mom is holding the coffee pot and begins to laugh. They are the elderly youngest daughters in a family of eleven children, her sister's parsimonious instinct comes as no surprise.

My mother reaches for my hand and covers it with hers on the coffee pot, resting both in her lap. Without words or forethought we travel together to a galley kitchen in Brooklyn with a single pane window looking into a brown-walled alley. The coffee pot sits on the stove, we both see it's clean white enamel, no garden paint. We feel the breeze as she passes, the woman whose kitchen we visit in memory; she reaches for the coffee pot. On the porch our hands touch where hers had been.

My mother didn't need the coffee pot, nor did I though it felt even more like a relative now. It was enough to let it transport us for a moment to that place where mothers and daughters get to be sometimes--where what matters is the connection and not the things, or the intertwining needs that so often engulf us.

Squeezing my hand affectionately, Mom rose off the porch, parted the grass near the bottom of the step and nestled the pot back into it's place.

> "Seems happy to be here," she said to me.
> "Me too," I grinned back at her, "me too.

On the Prowl

It is not Spring, but there is something hatching in the back of the cabinet; I am having a protracted war with pantry moths. I stalk them, brandishing a cracked and ancient plastic-mesh fly swatter, it's business end is sea-foam green. The wire handle, once coated in white vinyl is worn to bare metal. I bent the tip so that it hooks over the top of the cook-book shelf, utilitarian, ready to hunt and strike.

The moths intrude on my domestic equanimity. Their larvae get into packages of food, spoiling it. They compound the crime by leaving a web of detritus under the lid of the oatmeal container which puts me off hot cereal for a season, even two. Adding insult to injury, I have to wash every can, inspect every box, vacuum every corner. Still, there are more.

I am generally respectful of our insect neighbors. Living on the edge of a big forest makes me mindful that the inver-tebrate biomass in our neck of the woods has considerably greater mass than the human biomass does. We don't use pesticides in the garden. We give our kids screened bug houses so they can capture, watch, and release without tor-turing (however inadvertently). Our house even has a resident spider population that no one seems to mind so we cohabitate instead of eradicate. However, the moth invasion triggered an inner hunter-self I'd never encountered before: I stalk a critter that I have no intention of eating and want to kill even though it has not bitten me first.

This is not a kindly aspect of my personality. I am not, in any way, nice about it. I have now killed so many moths that I wonder at the karma of it. I set pheromone traps, then scan rooms, closets, nooks and crannies--fly swatter cocked and ready. Whap! There are tell-tale moth-colored velvet smudg-es on ceilings and walls that I will have to clean later; climb-ing on a stool with a damp paper towel--a process I have begun to think of as 'removing the evidence'. My family thinks I am a little nuts about the moth thing. I think this is preferable to being nuts about the worm thing when the next generation hatches. I hate wasting food a lot more than I hate wasting moths.

It started in the organic barley. Perhaps I should have frozen it instead of letting it sit in a paper bag for a month, waiting for stew-cooking weather. I went to pour barley into the simmering pot and stopped just in time; three moths flew out of the bag, blinking their wings into the light of day--into what my children have since dubbed 'the wrath of mom.' Before I could inspect the whole pantry I was obliged to embark on a week-long business trip. "Watch out for moths," I pleaded in vain to my family, "don't let them settle in."

As feared, I returned to discover many little sets of wings fluttering in the kitchen. I cleaned, sorted and reluctantly cast out food. A heyday for grain eaters at the compost pile. I washed shelves, cans, boxes and containers; moved things to the freezer and, finally, chucked that tin of Mediterranean figs in heavy syrup that had seemed like such a great idea when they were on sale during my last pregnancy (could it possibly be that many years?).

A few waning moth generations later, the swatter and I continue regular patrols. The children hear me coming up the stairs, muttering and thwacking my way through the house. They look askance when I enter a room, surreptitiously peeking to see if I am carrying my weapon. One or another of them is likely to comment that the moth thing is getting a little out of hand, "creepy," says the fifteen year old, her sisters nodding solemnly beside her. They want me to wash before I touch them. I tell them that our moths are clean, even though unwelcome, but still they want me kootie-free.

The barley is stored in the freezer now and I am slowly winning my crusade. I spend less time ranting around the house with a broken fly swatter, chasing tiny moths that flutter erratically between dark corners. My kids have learned how ruthless their mom can be, which could have an upside. I don't condone moth killing, really, but I'm beginning to appreciate that, as the intensity of life continues to ratchet up, this mama likes having an excuse to whack about the house for a bit of catharsis. Pantry moths beware.

Bear, Dog, Daughter

I have an old stuffed bear, a never favored but never discarded childhood friend that is unaccustomed to any kind of Velveteen Rabbit realness or love. One evening last summer the family dog ate most of it's head off then left it on the landing to be discovered by my eldest daughter, who was more distraught than I. She approached on tip toe in anticipation of my sorrow, holding the bear in her outstretched arm for me to see.

"Mom, I think Suki ate your bear, I'm so sorry."

Her eyes were wide with a collection of worries. Would I be sad about the bear being attacked? Would I get mad at the dog? Would I shoot the messenger? I have some complicated history with this bear and so my first response (which shocked my sensitive child's wide eyes even wider) was to laugh really, really hard in that slipping-the-usual-boundaries way that indicates all sorts of triggered responses which we mercifully imagine sailing over the heads of our children (trust me, they know when mama gets triggered). This bear, which I never named but nonetheless have kept, genuinely deserved to have it's head chewed on and it had taken decades to enjoy the sweetness of this peculiar satisfaction.

Beneath it's wooly brown fur the bear is not soft. It is stuffed with packed straw and it's limbs are held in a vulnerably open position with an infrastructure of stiff unbendable wire. It has marble eyes, a small hard plastic nose, and it's head is turned permanently to the side so it only sees in one direction. It was made to be frozen in this uncomfortable position and for all these years I have felt more pity for it than love.

A stuffed bear was the holiday gift I *most* longed for when I was 8. I can still taste the disappointment that stung my heart when I'd pulled away the wrapping from the bear-shaped gift, swallowing back dismay. Had my parents somehow misunderstood? My lonely eight year old self genuinely longed for something soft to carry and snuggle. I had asked specifically for a stuffed teddy bear. I unwrapped this stiff unyielding thing; over forty years later I am still awed that my otherwise astute parents had chosen such an inflexible interpretation of a comfort object.

Eventually, grudgingly, I came to love this bear; even as I came to understand that my parents misguided attempts to meet my needs were acts intended to nurture. The bear has traveled with me all this time, packed, unpacked, set on a shelf, and occasionally rescued from a tug-o-war between my three children. Since it only has the talent of looking in one direction, they made this bear the lookout on the stairs when the other bears were up to mischief.

I explained my laughter to my daughter by telling her the story of how I'd wanted something soft to snuggle and she rolled her eyes at my parents' woeful misunderstanding. I told how this bear would have been a goner if I'd had a dog growing up because I'd have let it eat the darn bear and so I would not scold this dog for the damage done. Besides, a real dog that loves you is much better comfort than any stuffed animal. She nodded and took the bear away, tucked gently under an arm.

The next morning my daughter brought me the bear, re-paired, with a newly configured head. It is blind now, it's nose got lost in translation and one ear is a transplant. It is still stiff and hard, wire and straw. For the first time this bear, restored by my daughter's tender hands, felt like a true gift. I was able to reach for it, to thank her; to feel uncompli-cated love and hold it close without the metal tang of remem-bered disappointment rolling across my tongue.

Nowadays the bear sits on a high shelf near my writing desk, still a mischief lookout. Having survived the dog, it has ad-opted elder statesman status in the hierarchy of family trea-sures. I swear that it's blind eyes follow the dog with suspi-cion. I sit and stare at it often, instead of being a reminder of my own childhood sorrow it has new purpose, reassuring me that mending is always a possibility. One thing about mothering that always takes me by surprise is my kids' ability to see and understand my vulnerabilities. This is not the first old hurt one of their kindnesses has repaired in me, though it is perhaps the sweetest mending I have ever witnessed.

Resistance of the Heart
Against Business as Usual

I'm driving along on a beautiful morning, ignoring radio news, all of a sudden -- tears stream down my face. Not listening, but my heart hears. Bombs, children, mayhem. The ambient distress is raining on my parade -- it's the war.

I've been crying in the car a lot. I am a glass-full person, not usually prone to driving through a sea of tears. And because moms talk while dropping children off at dance class, I know I'm not the only unaccustomed weeper on the road. If life is always this hard why is it suddenly making me cry?

In February, 2003 I marched with my children and twenty million other human beings to stop American military aggression. Many winters later I still struggle to understand how we failed to halt the machines of war. I've been dissenting from and grappling with reality ever since. The election of President Obama changed everything and nothing, though it did make the work ahead seem more possible to accomplish.

Almost a decade later the war in Afghanistan drags on. If more of us become aware of how the war affects us, we might become less complacent about allowing it to continue. America's wars: on terror, on drugs, on science, besmirch the ideals of democracy. I long to hear, instead, radio stories celebrating improved international cooperation and coordinated response to climate disruption.

Is it too audacious to hope we can pull off a coordinated response and land ourselves a sustainable future? I cannot imagine the world twenty five years from now, it makes me uncomfortable to try. How much more audacious we will need to be in order to act. It will require, to quote Bread and Puppet Theater's suggestion, "Resistance of the Heart Against Business as Usual".

Twice in recent years I've come upon animal bones working out of the soil. First, seven small mammalian vertebrae, growing mossy, scattered on a high ridge in western Massachusetts. Next, the earth returned bleached remnants of a sea-bird's wing, pushing up near the ocean in Maine. I carried them away home, where I can touch their purpose, wing and spine.

Sitting up too late at my desk I pick up three vertebrae, shake and tumble them in my cupped hand, listening to the click clack of their relation to me. In the best stories bones are knocked together by hags, gamblers or old gods, all with the power to influence nations. Would that I could lay claim to being more than an ordinary lady with no hero in tow, no powers to bend world events or mend global weather. Looked at straight on the vertebrae appear as delicate dragon heads breathing back to me the ghost-fire of some animal's raw spinal impulse. We are, I think, made of the same stuff, bone and blood and the fire of intelligence...stone, water, atoms from stars.

If I believed in some entity outside myself suitable to pray to, to beseech and humbly implore: that the war be ended, it's victims healed, the land repaired, soldier-souls mended... if that kind of believing were possible for me then my prayer would be ceaseless.

Instead, what I do believe in, is you. In ideas, community, the power of individuals to do good in ordinary ways, combining to make a greater good. This river of tears we've been weeping is an honor to the earth. Our grief about climate change and war is not something to hide away until our bones, stripped clean, work themselves out of the soil again.

We are in the deep dark of the year, a time to shelter the fires that burn in us. I know that moles will spend the winter eating the roots of my perennials, mice will lunch on new bulbs

I planted. Life is full of these subterranean disappointments. I won't be surprised to learn the new President has flaws or that we need more community organizers to make things work better, again.

There's a story I've begun telling myself in the car about a lame duck Emperor who has no clothes and his successor, an ordinary man with no hero in tow who will rely on other ordinary people to build, together, a sustainable future. The tale unfolds, the miles spin by, from somewhere across the radio signals I hear the click clack of my relation to everything: it makes me cry. I'll whisper this story to the stars through the dark nights coming, about how our tears can nurture the roots of audacious hope and the fire in our hearts can resist business as usual.

2020 Addendum:
Plus ça change, plus c'est la même chose.
(the more things change, the more they stay the same)

Frog Lady

The first fine Sunday in April I was basking in the garden, drenched in the euphoria of sun-on-skin when my middle kid popped the bubble, shouting, "MomMomMom! One frog and EGGS in the pond! And we found a salamander too, it's climbing my arm, you wanna hold it?"

I was not surprised by her discovery; a few minutes before I had startled my own first frog. We'd sat blinking at one another for a bit until I moved along the row to give it privacy again. Now, my daughter's salamander crossed to my hand, looking up hopefully. I handed it back.

"Don't keep it too long," I reminded her, "mostly it wants to be exploring."

"I know, I know, isn't it cool?" she called, already running off.

My children know that I treasure these early Spring visits with our amphibian neighbors. When I was little there was a small pond near home where we'd skate in winter and mount muddy expeditions the rest of the year. I pestered the boys, who mostly wanted to see how many ways they could blow up frogs, and tattled when they escalated to using M-80's for depth charges. I may have sealed my fate with the local thugs but the frogs were appreciative. I spent the hottest summer hours on my belly in the cool grass, happily observing pond life.

I grew up to be a woman of many trades. Apparently the early pond-watching paid off and one of my job titles is 'frog lady.' Now please, this is very different from being a 'cat lady.' I know from personal experience because I once met a cat lady and her 60(!) cats, and I am not like that at all. I prefer the beings I am 'lady' to, to live in their own digs -- not mine. I am happy with respectfully distant encounters, only touching for assistance (i.e. liberation from 4 year olds who are reminded again not to squeeze so hard). But I didn't know that I had crossed the line and become an official frog lady until my affinity for the frog-legged prompted a stranger to ask, "You're one of those frog ladies, aren't you?"

I'd been driving home late on a wet spring night. I had to swerve often to avoid the small froggy shapes bobbing, arms akimbo, through the mist illuminated by my headlights. The frog I stopped to rescue appeared as a glisteny-green mass sitting very still in the middle of a three-way rural intersection. Unaware that I was observed by a human passerby I stopped my car, doused the headlights and set the flashers. The air smelled of Spring; sweet earth, leaf mould and worms. I stood inhaling the night a few seconds before speaking aloud to the frog.

"Hey friend, it's not safe here. Better to move along," I suggested. It blinked. It was as big as my hand.

"No, really," I pleaded. "This isn't a good place for a frog – get going now." I stepped a little closer. It leaned a bit forward so I came nearer and bent towards it.

"Time to move along friend, the cars are big and they can't see you," I confided.

It blinked again, then in three exuberant arcing jumps it landed at the side of the road. As it continued hopping away the new grass let loose droplets of mist that sparkled in the street light, marking it's progress.

I turned to go and was startled by a figure standing in the shadows across the way. "Oh, hello, I didn't see you," I stammered, embarrassed at being caught talking to a frog.

That's when she said it, "You're one of those frog ladies, aren't you?"

I replied with a little shrug. "I guess maybe I am," I giggled, charmed that this is something a person can grow up and become: one of those frog ladies.

I climbed back into my car still pleased with this new revelation of my purpose in life. And maybe looking out for the welfare of our amphibian neighbors is a catchy thing. These days, if my husband is driving the family home on a warm wet night in Spring, one of our daughters is as likely as I am to remind him, "watch out for the frogs."

Early Morning Minuet

My teenage daughter's school bus comes at 6:45 a.m. For this mom, a slacker way before there was a hip word for it, 6:45 a.m. is for special occasions - not every day appearances. When school began in September she took my quirks in stride and willingly rose alone at 6:00 a.m. All on her own she puttered in the bathroom, dug in the dryer for clean jeans and softly thumped her way downstairs. I'd gratefully snooze until I heard the front door close behind her and, confident she'd made her bus, rest until it was time to get the sibs up.

As the mercury dipped towards winter it started to be dark in the morning: one more reason to stay in bed. To my dismay, this self-proclaimed 'big kid' wanted company in the dusky shadows at the end of the driveway where she waits for the bus. She is my frontier child, always showing me the edge I need to step past next, teaching me how to let go. I, who for years managed never to keep a job I had to arrive at before 10:00 a.m., have finally surrendered to the necessity of being an early riser.

Waking at 6:00 a.m. has become a habit most appreciated by the cat, who unlike me, wants to play. I oblige her by groping open my daughter's door to be let in with me, and we climb through the piles to the bed where the cat jumps up while I pretend to be an alarm clock. "Beep-beep," I call into the pattern of her soporific respiration, "beep-beep" again, as I tug the blanket a few inches off her shoulder. She smiles up at me, "beep" bleats my lamb in the small voice of sleep. My willingness to forgo first-light dreams is rewarded by this daily glimpse of her waking moments. She sits up and since no one is watching, melts against my flank, resting on her way to the day. I rub her back. She scritches the kitty. It is too early for words.

Downstairs, we still don't talk much. I make tea, she reads over the cereal bowl, gathers homework, brushes hair. She might tell me about a friend or add to the list of reasons she dislikes her social studies teacher. I am not well-formed enough, so early, to do more than cliche parenting; I nod and smile, ask what she wants for dinner, grumble that she never wears socks, and insist that she go back upstairs for a sweater. For thirty minutes or so we keep company; she doesn't have to share or wait for a louder sister to finish first.

When I was considering having a third child it never occurred to me that I would eventually be required to attempt the peculiar physics of being three moms in one. This wasn't an issue when they were little: three kids within a six year spread--it seemed like I could manage their spectrum of development and needs well enough. It was possible to integrate a sort of all-purpose-mama that worked for everybody.

Nowadays it's a lot harder to be one-mom-fits-all: an eight year old requires a different model of mommy than an eleven or fourteen year old does. Getting the knack of shifting gears fast enough, at the right moment, and smoothly...well, my daughters will concur that I'm still on the learning curve and expect to be burning out clutches, and metaphors, for some time yet.

Our early rising, frontier, first born child knows she can count on her slacker mom to get synchronized with any schedule, eventually. We are learning the steps to this parent-adolescent dance as we go along. It's a minuet of letting go and welcoming return, of comprehending and responding to each other's changing needs. Every day I hope to dance well enough to achieve a certain grace, to nurture her lingering girlhood and simultaneously foster her independent woman-self. To keep me mindful of the dance, each schoolday offers this pleasure: I squeeze her hand lightly just before she gets on the bus, feel her squeeze back, and savor the distinct sensation as her able fingers slip away from mine.

Craggy Dancing

Life in a female body involves surrender to years of bio-physical processes over which we have little or no personal control. The chemical changes that are triggered in women's bodies by ovulation may represent our essential connection to the web of life but, as I remember it, being female, adolescent and hormonal really sucked. No one warned me that being forty-five and hormonal would exponentially suck.

If you ask me, peri-menopause is way too perky a name for such a craggy state of body-mind. Now, just as my three daughters become ripely adolescent, I am hitting my own hormonal stride. Or is that slide...? Yeah, definitely sliding. I don't think I could bear to feel more vulnerable, but since 'the only way out is through' I may as well get on with it.

My periods still come like clockwork but after all these years the new power of PMS to bend mind and emotion takes me by surprise. The premenstrual wee-hours anxiety segues into daytime disquietude; the voices of my discontent begin to sing as round and round we go. Swirling in the disharmony of competing inner needs and biological processes is wearing me out but I have to laugh, realizing how bored I am by versions of the same old tune. What a hullabaloo!

Sometimes my blood seems old and used up. I never aspired to conventional beauty; I don't wear makeup. I am naive enough to have been genuinely shocked when I figured out that most of my friends have not gone grey because they dye their hair. In middle age, living with daughters whose youth oozes everywhere, it's easy to accept that the standard of beauty our culture so avidly consumes is not a benchmark I'll attain.

There is a French expression, jolie-laid, which roughly translates as beautiful-ugly. It describes someone or something that exists outside of conventional beauty, is instead made more interesting by an innate and transcendent

contradiction to ideals of beauty. Or something so ugly that it has the power to fascinate us so thoroughly that 'ugly' becomes irrelevant. Jolie-laid is a state of physical being I aspire to because, nowadays, young men in shops call me ma'am and my kids say I'm old. My shredded vanity is the biggest joke of all. There is no way to hide my flaws and, still, I find myself in front of the mirror making sure whatever I'm wearing drapes to my satisfaction. Drapes!

Peri-menopause is a period of transition. Parts of ourselves are left behind or chucked out or, I confess, burned in the fire-circle in the front yard when no one else is home. It is hard to know sometimes what needs leaving and what wants keeping, or at least tucking away for reconsideration. There is a small sign on the front door of my house that reads: chaos is the natural order of the universe, welcome. Most people miss it on the way in and I have to repaint it periodically because it fades away. The equivalent of saying 'enter at your own risk', it is my little mantra, a daily reassurance that life is supposed to feel like this right now.

I am tired of inventing myself again and again, yet this seems to be what life requires. There are roles and layers, facets and permutations. There are elements and theories and, even in chaos, rules and laws.

Dancing between my growing children, their ailing grandparents, and all the changes of middle age, I look for balance. On better days I find some, and perch, teetering, until I can laugh about being vulnerable without snagging on the barbs of a too-sharp tongue, or being swamped in shifting hormonal tides or the black backwaters of ennui.

The room where I write and make art is home to collections: small plastic items, bird nests, words, pine cones, old metal bits, bark, and stones. Cigar boxes, feathers, odd tools, doll parts. Among other things. I moved recently, a process which requires a great deal of touching, a slow consideration of objects that hold layers of association and meaning. The times and experiences that comprise my life seem strung like pearls, luminescent orbs knotted in random order on a thrumming silken line played out into the wind.

The new room has a west facing window that opens on a long view across an expanse of forest canopy and beyond the tallest towers in town--meeting the horizon miles away. Looking out is restorative. Hawks rise in thermal spirals. Crows make a daily pilgrimage to roost in a neighbor's tall oaks. I remember my place and it is safe. When friends ask how I am, I reply, "well enough," grateful to mostly mean it even if I am sliding.

So what if the hormonal soup I'm slogging through as my body ages seems specifically designed to make all of my relationships more complicated. So what if my untidy craggy dancing requires backwards as well as forward motion to finesse the swirling intricacies of peri-menopause. I may not be aging gracefully and it's certainly not pretty, but if this is the price of maintaining an essential connection to the web of life, then I'll keep up this craggy dance.

Cruising for Chairs

I confess. I've been shopping at a discount furniture outlet famous for commercials on late-night T.V. The lacquered Italian bedroom ensemble with ornate mirrors, "only $799, come on down!" seems diminished in real life.

Two previous trips had not yielded the right chair for my studio. The first visit left me deflated, like I'd been sent up from the thrift store minor league to the 'big show' and struck out. On the second visit I made the fatal error of wandering upstairs where golf shirts and tans abound; the high-end sales force is altogether less wrinkled. They left me alone as soon as they saw my wrinkles, intuiting a basement shopper gone astray. I found the chair of my dreams: a wide-bodied chenille chaise in wine and forest tones. I climbed in, allowed my fantasy five minutes to play itself out, laughed at the price-tag, then gave up and drove home.

On the third visit I duck the eager basement sales team and scan the room to assess any personal resonance with the furniture on hand. New deliveries arrive every day. What if my chair isn't scheduled for the floor until next week? What if I don't "come on down" on the right day? Could I miss my rendezvous with furniture destiny?

I try the most likely looking chairs, rejecting each for being flawed; strange color, too deep, stiff fabric. I'm testing a Naugahyde rocking recliner (overkill?) when I see it. The room fades, my personal soundtrack cues, my new chair glows. I approach, nonchalantly running my hand across the pillows. It's not scratchy. It is also flawed: the feet are loose, it's poorly made. But it has armrest wings that bring to mind the classy fins on a 1957 Chevy Bel Air. Finally, a chair a body can nap in--cruising the dreamscapes in style.

A strategically savvy saleslady catches my eye. I nod, she heads my way.

"I think I've found my chair," I tell her, my legs propped over the armrest. The seat is wide, meeting the requirement to fit me and a kid with a book. It's covered in dusky blue faux chenille, it's a cheap chair and the upholstery won't hold up to living room forts, but in my studio it will serve well for reading and naps.

"It comes with this ottoman," the saleslady teases, pushing forward a matching foot rest, on wheels! I'm hooked but keep my poker face.

"How much?"

"Well, with the regular markdown plus today's special ten percent, it's $234.00. We don't deliver from the basement and you have to pick up within twenty four hours." She's recited the terms. I am prepared to pay more for a chair to nap in. I squint in to the game, thinking about whether I should haggle or just take it and be glad.

"This is my third trip in two months," I confide. "I was getting worried I'd become a regular, but I've browsed enough. Thanks." We do the paper work and shake amicably.

Before bringing my car to the loading dock I detour upstairs again. I want to sit one last time on that chaise. It is as delicious as I remembered but I feel no pang of regret, no sense that I'm getting less than what I want or need. Mostly, I'm relieved that I haven't spent more than I can afford.

Out back at the loading dock there is a constant flow of furniture being pulled out of the warehouse and stuffed into or roped on top of vehicles. I take delivery from a big man with a bigger smile who, despite my confidence, is skeptical about squeezing the chair in the back of my van. I make adjustments, it fits with inches to spare. I grin.

"I'm good with spatial relationships," I tell him, adding a thank you. Then I'm off home where every one will

54

try my new chair, see all it's flaws and also understand, (without my needing to explain), why I bought it anyway.

Fat Mama

5-20-99
It is after midnight. I'm wiping away the goo in the sink,
putting the drain strainer into the dishwasher along with the
stinky sponges, uncharacteristically cleaning the underside
of the faucet, about to sanitize the handle on the refrigerator
door...I stop and sit to write instead.

This afternoon my seven year old daughter came home from
school saying she is "different" but unable to define how.
"They tease me mommy," she says from around her thumb,
which is perpetually in her mouth, which I am perpetually
asking her to remove so that I can understand her. "What
do they say?" I ask, distracted by the baby until she answers,
"They say my mom is fat."

"Well, that's true," I tell her, carefully neutral, "how do you
feel when they say that?"

"Really embarrassed," she says, and I see she is hurting even
to tell me this much. Something intangible has changed between us, the pain others cause her is because of me: mother
a liability rather than a champion. My body size is affecting
her social life. She loves me. There is a new shadow in our
shared landscape.

"When they say that to you just tell them 'So what!'. I am fat,
sweetheart, and that's ok. I'm not ashamed," I lie, because I
don't want her to feel ashamed of me or of herself.

So, I clean my kitchen out of grief. I've been up since 5 a.m.
and will wake up tomorrow at 5 a.m. I don't want to go to
bed with these words stuffed down or pinching in my sleep.
Mothering can make me so weary some days but has never
hurt like this before. I am angry. I feel rage at a culture that
so despises fat people and then inflicts that hate on little girls
who turn it in on themselves.

Tomorrow I will send a note to her teacher, we will discuss the teasing. My girl and I will learn to face this with each other in an honest way. I can not change the truth of being fat. I cannot protect her from the cruelty of our culture. But I can teach her to be like a duck, to let the hate roll off. I can oil her feathers, ensure her wings are strong, teach her to stand her ground and help her to appreciate the difference between a convenient play mate and a real friend. And maybe when she is grown up some I will show her these late night words, and she will know that I am sorry for the hurts.

6-15-04

Last week the third and youngest daughter came off the school bus cranky and climbed into my lap; a long day in kindergarten I figured. But there was something more, a question she started to ask, then stopped with a resigned "never mind," but sighed and started and stopped again, as if she was picking at a mental scab that had a certain sharp hurt under it. I waited, stroking her cheek. Finally the words came, barely audible, "some kids drew a picture of me and you and they made your body this wide," she murmured, holding her hands wider than any paper size available in kindergarten, "they keep asking why my mom is fat and it is really bugging me."

Five years have passed and I am still fat. So I offer the same advice I gave when her oldest sister was a first grader, "tell them that's true, so what, and then let it go. Good mom's come in all shapes and sizes." She decides we should read books instead of talking.

I didn't take up the cleanser or stay up past my bedtime and I won't talk to the teacher this time around. But I am frustrated. Americans are so afraid of being ugly that it is still acceptable to judge and poke fun at fat folks. I will explain to my five year old that size is just another variable in the amazing array of human kind, that there are still cultures in this world where fat women are revered and desired. I want to teach her to face down mean people with honesty and an unflappable demeanor.

Maybe you can teach your kids what I teach mine: that it takes all kinds and sizes to make the world such an interesting place and that being fat doesn't make someone stupid or jolly or less worthy of other's esteem. I am learning that the shadows in the landscapes I share with my daughters shift with the seasons and sometimes even with the time of day. And that reading together is always a good remedy for a rough afternoon at kindergarten.

Published 4/06 - Daily Hampshire Gazette

Hands

The latest round of high tech imaging of my deteriorating spine has had an unexpected side effect. My husband is afraid that I might break if he touches me in some inexplicably wrong way he could not possibly anticipate. This is not a surface fear, it is not overt or even (especially not even) spoken. Instead it is articulated through his finger tips; I cannot earn back their trust of my resilience. After twenty five years of being touched by one man, this sensory change is more frightening to me than the growing numbness in my legs or the list of other physical changes I can expect to experience as my neurological disease progresses.

What comes through my husband's finger tips is worry. It used to be just the pleasure of feeling my skin.

There are so many things that change, and don't, in a long marriage. This one thing, being touched with confidence, should not change. I still want his hands on me, firmly tracing contours and curves. The same hands that burnished my flank through my twenties and soothed my brow during childbirth, now, in middle age, have gained a hesitation.

I want that hesitation to go. It reminds me that I am flawed under my skin, inside my bones. I cannot fix or cut away these flaws, though we sometimes try to make small corrections. My orthopedic surgeon, when I ask, explains his personal theory about people like me, whose spines degenerate without exacerbating injury, wondering aloud if I may have a genetic something that effects the way the body builds collagen, "maybe when we know more" he sighs. For now he advises me to expect change and make the most of the mobility I have.

I had a body that delighted in the pleasure inherent in itself. A body that could feel all the places a hand might touch. Now there are blank areas where sensation is indistinct, like trying to feel through the sensory equivalent of snow on a tv

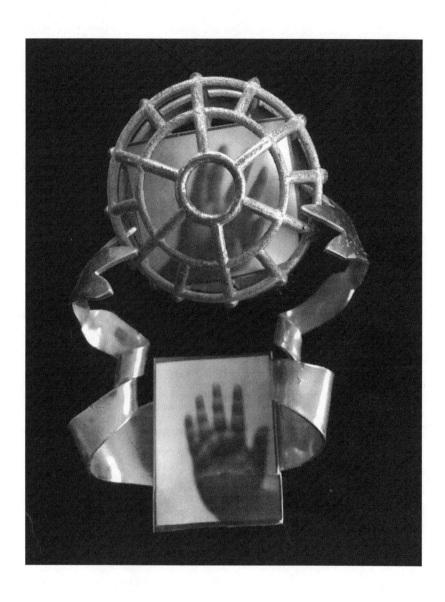

screen. Now there are repercussions to touch. Quadrants of my skin tingle sharply, the brush of a hand triggering an unpleasant buzz back to the nerve root.

Talking about having a disability sometimes entails casting modesty aside, so I will tell you that after spine surgery a number of years ago I found that at a certain stage of sexual stimulation I crossed a sensational threshold into nothingness. After a little panic and some long thinking, redirecting and practice, I have developed a new cascade of feeling. It almost works if I concentrate and then don't concentrate at just the right moment. I am too old to be surprised that sex is such a coyote trickster, and I don't care so much about orgasm any more, but when my partner is worried he could harm me if he moves wrong -- well sometimes you just have to give up, lay there, and laugh till it stops hurting.

I am learning to navigate this changing relationship with myself but the lessons don't come easy. I have no map for exploring the shifting terrain of my physicality. I like to imagine there are wonders I have yet to discover.

Like many middle aged women I mourn youth and beauty. Not in a vain way--but I hadn't expected my sensual life to fade away like this. I can accept the incremental steps of honoring who I see in the mirror but, when I am most honest with the woman looking back at me, I am haunted by questions that reveal an aching vulnerability. Will my husband unlearn this hesitation in his hand? Or will it spread quietly to his eyes and then his lips? I keep wanting to tell him that only my heart will break, not my bones, if this becomes the status quo. Fear catches the words.

This is the aspect of my condition that I cannot quantify when my doctor asks me to list the five things that hurt the most. This loss hurts the most but there is no medicine for it. I am lonely because being touched no longer feels good; lonely even though my life is rich in friendship. For a time in my teens I was homeless. Lately I feel like pain has put me on the outside of "normal" in a way similar to homelessness. I am made a little bit but perpetually a vagabond because I cannot get comfortable in my own skin.

Recently, walking in the woods I found a sunny spot and curled up on the forest floor. I thought it would be restful for just a while to be a little animal in a big woods. I made a nest of my coat and lay there, letting the forest touch me in a time-lapse dream, connecting me elementally between sky and root, stone and bone, rain and tears. I lay there until this wild need for hands feeling good on my skin had wept itself quiet again and left me empty of the needing.

Sometimes, I wake in the middle of the night and lay listening to my husband snore, keeping rhythm with the tree frogs outside. When I roll him to stop the snoring a hand reaches out to me. While he sleeps this hand remembers only how soft and familiar I feel. His touch is tender, resting an arm across my side and warming my stomach with light fingers. I curl myself around this gift, this hand that remembers my youth and can still feel the pulse of love in me.

'Hands' was originally published in the disability journal Breath & Shadow and then again in 'Dozen: the best of Breath and Shadow,' edited by Chris Kuell (2016).

Sardines

My daughter attends a high school eighteen miles from home, I drive her every morning. She stands in front of a full fridge, tells me there is never anything to eat, then lets me know she needs a new trench coat for her Fall wardrobe. If there are pots in the kitchen sink she fills her glass in the bathroom; it has never occurred to her to wash the pots. Don't get me wrong, she is a great kid, has caring friends, reads widely, holds up her end of a conversation. I have nothing to kvetch about.

I know it's cliche for us older folks to go on about trudging up hill through thigh-deep snow both ways to school when we were young, but I do it anyway because I like her to know how good she has it. When I was sixteen I was sleeping on a storage loft in a leaking wooden garage in a back yard in California, cleaning house in exchange for the place to crash, doing odd jobs for odd cash, panhandling for dinner and a movie. My teenage compadres included the genius homeless on the cusp of the Aquarian age and post-trauma Viet Nam vets watching the war news from El Salvador, their tired eyes lit blue by the bar's TV screen light. It wasn't high school, but I got a unique education in that halcyon time before AIDS and crack turned the streets mean.

I did not have a bed in a room in a house with heat and parents who provided the foods that I most liked to eat. I did not have someone who rubbed my neck when I had a head-ache or who listened when I found out something new about how the world works. For me it was more about how to work the world. Which leads me in the usual back door fashion to sardines.

Good protein. You can go a long way on sardines. They are cheap, you get bang for the buck. With cucumber and pita bread, also cheap, you have a meal. Add cream cheese and you have three squares. I don't like them very well because they remind me of being homeless and sleeping in a garage. They also remind me of surviving. And of what hungry tastes like. There is always a tin of sardines in my cabinet. I eat them when no one else is home -- when I worry about my children being too soft to know how to work the world and to keep my own sense of irony honed and useful.

The tight sense of lack on the wind tells me we are heading into hard times. An 85 year old friend who remembers Great Depression bread lines told me recently that we have no idea how what's coming will change our lives. I'm confident I can survive hard times but I don't know how to protect my family from the supply-side unpleasantness the country seems poised at the edge of.

I find myself stocking up on odd items: toilet paper and sanitary napkins, hydrogen peroxide, honey, dried beans. Imagining what I might miss most or trade best if commodities become harder to get. The other day while unpacking groceries I turned to put away the sardines and was surprised to find three tins already packed humbly on the shelf. Apparently I am unconsciously laying-in a supply of good protein.

In my youth I met a lot of conspiracy theorists; street people, troubadours, barefoot saints and veterans of foreign wars, all thinking on the fringe of possible realities. I carried a pocket of salt to protect myself from thinking like them. Thirty years later and much to my dismay, their wacky future-picture projections have turned eerily accurate. I am angry that the world I worked out for myself -- the one with a home, family and a retirement account -- is so vulnerable to the political and corporate machinations of power brokers whose social priorities I wholeheartedly dissent from.

Years ago, when it became obvious the war would go on and on, I told my kids at dinner one night that I was sorry. I explained that the world was changing in ways I could not have anticipated when deciding to conceive them in the

1990's. Then, I had thought we were finally realizing Dr. King's hoped for trajectory, where the arc of history bends towards justice. Now, I told them, I expected times to slowly get harder and perhaps even remarkably hard and that we should look on these slow times as a period of grace in which to appreciate what plenty looks like. An apology which sailed right over the heads of my children who were 5, 8 and 11 at the time.

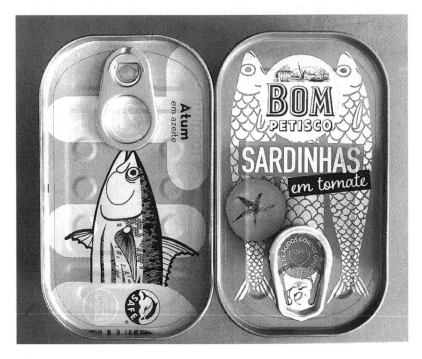

Lately, the eldest daughter listens to the news and shoots me worried glances. I cannot promise her the world she was born into, the one with polar bears, hopes for nuclear disarmament, and a full pantry. My daughter sees the shadows of my life experience in the backs of my eyes, shimmering like a school of sardines darting in response to the deep currents of time. She is a high school junior and wants to go to college; it's become hard to get student loans. What is the best way to foster her independence and these early passes at a search for meaning in life? If she wants to move out in two years what kind of entry level job will provide enough income to cover housing, utilities, transportation and food?

What about health care?

Funny how old songs gain new currency as times change. The other day I heard my daughter humming that Joni Mitchell tune "They Paved Paradise", singing along with the radio, "don't it always seem to go that you don't know what you've got till it's gone..." There are deep currents shifting in the national soul, Americans have reached out to grab ahold of the arc of history and bend it back towards justice. The election results won't save the polar bears or end the war, or help my small rural town manage with shrinking budgets. As much as we choose change in the voting booth every four years or so, change is also choosing us. I suspect that in spite of the security of a family home, my daughter may have to come of age just as I did, by learning to hold her nose and eat sardines.

Putting On My Mary Pants

My mom called me this morning at around 7am. Which is actually ok since I was sitting awake in my hospital bed feeling really sad about the predicament of my spine. I had a double surgery the other day and will need another within a month or two. Recovery for spine surgery is a bitch, but having another procedure waiting in the wings is plain overwhelming. It is not just being brave enough to endure the indignities of hospitalization, or mustering the courage to try stairs when you don't feel your legs are completely on board. It is the necessity of constant vigilance on your own behalf. I've been begging for a real stool softener for two days, and finally got the timing right and a nurse was able to get the doctor to order it. I've got two long incisions on my spine but for the moment being able to poo is my biggest problem because it keeps me from being able to go home. And I really want to go home.

Chalk it up to lousy DNA, my spine is a train wreck of unprovoked degeneration. Sometimes it requires surgical repair. Once you have had spine surgery, subsequent procedures come as no surprise, but there is a dark side to knowing what you are getting yourself into. You have lost the mystery and unconsciousness of what comes next. The work of finding your feet again, the rearrangement of your balance and reflexes. The long slow days ahead of being gimpy and medicated. All of this causes me some dread.

As usual, the only way out is through. So while I was on the phone with my mom, I told her, "I am putting on my Mary pants." And she knew just what I meant. Mary was her mother-in-law. A stoic, bright woman who liked to play scrabble, gin rummy, and pinochle; she taught me how to lose gracefully and celebrated when I won. She had a way of getting through the hard parts of life with straightforward determination. Mary was the person who taught me to give up my seat on the bus to someone, any one, whose feet were more tired than mine. She taught me the value of being a friendly and open person. She taught me good manners and how to be nicer all around. It is hard for me to surrender to being a patient in the bed; and in the hospital, all of these skills are useful.

When I need that kind of steady-on mojo in my life, I call it "putting on my Mary pants."

At the moment, I would like to be any place else but here. I would like to not have the spine I have. I would like to not have to advocate tirelessly in order to get my stuck gut addressed. But this is where I am, and this is what lies ahead. I am so glad my mom knew what I meant, that I am going to tuck into getting myself through this with pragmatic optimism, and some moxie from my Gram.

Spring Rant

I don't know about you, but I am really ready for the hundredth monkey to wash her yam! I am ready for humanity to get it: to embrace peace and justice, to make potable water, clean food, adequate shelter, health care, and sustainable employment available to everyone equally. I am, I'm ready, so why the delay? What in the name of Jane is taking us so long?

It is abundantly evident, as Dwight D. Eisenhower warned in April of 1953, that "Every gun that is made, every warship launched, every rocket fired signifies, in the final sense, a theft from those who hunger and are not fed, those who are cold and are not clothed. This world in arms is not spending money alone. It is spending the sweat of its laborers, the genius of its scientists, the hopes of its children." Ike did more than warn about the famed military industrial complex--he made it clear that we are always making this choice between war and the common good, they cannot be mutually served.

It has been equally evident, since Rachel Carson's 'Silent Spring' was published in the 1960's, that climate disruption is the obvious result of our blatantly corrupt use of energy and disposal of waste. We have warmed and poisoned the planetary soup. We all know it, even as we sip from the gas pumps and power-plants day after day. We grumble at what it costs us, all the while ignoring the real costs of environmental degradation. It is inevitably our own human environment that we endanger, everywhere is our own backyard.

In February of 2003, millions of people the world over marched simultaneously for peace. I thought, "surely now the hundredth monkey has her yam gripped firmly, ready to dip it in the stream." I hoped there was some possibility of realizing my personal concept of Rapture; a heaven on earth where every one is Chosen, global warming is safely neutralized, and 'swords into plowshares' is the sign of the times.

I am ready for locally sustainable food production and supply chains; for energy decisions made on the basis of regional resources and conditions as well as cleanliness, sustainability and renewability. I'm ready for everyone's environmental awareness to include the scope and well-being of all life on earth, in all eco systems. I am ready for humanity to understand that it must, first, do no harm.

I am ready to smash the patriarchy and dismantle white supremacy. I am ready to return land and restore sovereignty to Indigenous communities. I am ready for democracy to build again in the United Sates of America: for the eradication of electronic voting machines and the return to paper ballot and pencil--voting tools I can be certain accurately reflect my choice. I am ready for elected officials to be accountable to their constituents instead of to lobbyists. I am ready for nations to cease warring; my nation, the USA, should stop first. And apologize.

Well, Y'all, even though my arm gets tired, I'm gonna keep washing my yam until all you other monkeys are washing along with me. One of us is the blessed hundredth monkey – even if it takes a hundred thousand million to be washing together before she gets the hang of it and shakes her furry yam-holding hand in the water, too. Even if there is NO hundredth monkey and never was. I am ready. How about you?

And before you tell me there is no monkey, yeah I know. If you want to fuss about it, then the answer to the question, "100th monkey?" is here:
http://en.wikipedia.org/wiki/100th_Monkey

Dura Mater ~ Tough Mother

I had a date with my husband the other night, we went for dinner and to see a band at our local pub, an after dark outing which has become rare for me. The food was great and The Pistoleros were tight, the drummer even flirted with me from the stage. I sat so that I could see the players and also got to watch one especially good dancer express the joy of being in their body. Honestly though, as my disability progresses going out to hear a band seems more like watching life from the sidelines. The blues that linger with me for days after is one of the reasons I don't go out much.

I move pretty well for a person with a spinal cord injury. I don't use a wheelchair (yet) and in the close quarters of a bar I opted to leave my cane in the car so no one would trip over it. I cannot get up to dance. If the music is good enough that I can't sit still (and it was) then I can dance in my chair if I gently move only my arms or only my feet, but not with vigor and not both at the same time to avoid bruising my dura mater.

Another reason I don't go out much is the inevitability of the following conversation, that may happen repeatedly:

Person X: How nice to see you, you're moving well!

Me: Thank you. Nice to see you too, I'm well enough.

Person X: You must be getting better.

Me: No, I have a spinal cord injury that is progressively worse. I am not better, and I am well enough.

Person X: (discomforted by bad news and backing away) Well, this is good then. Ok, see you soon.

I love that people want me to feel better. And. There is so much more going on in my life than my disability and health

issues! I wish you would ask me about the workshop I am designing or my new book, or about the chapel where the last funeral service I conducted took place (because that was pretty darn cool).

And please don't be disappointed with my head shake 'no' when you've maneuvered through the crowd reaching out your arms to see if I will dance with you. I would love to dance with you, but my central nervous system says otherwise and the repercussions of my succumbing to your invitation could, really, be that I fall and cannot walk again. So I am cautious, and it can look from the outside like rejection.

And after a while people don't ask how you are or invite you to dance. And that is ok. I am a tough mother.

Dura mater is the thick membrane that protects all the flow of intelligence between your brain and your body, your breath and your blood, your motion and your stillness... my dura mater is torn, leaks, and has places where bone pokes in hard. There is not a cure, there is not a surgery or a pill, there is not a mitigating diet or an exercise program (especially not that, since moving can be dangerous). There is no fix. There is the ongoing conversation with super-duper qualified orthopedic and neuro surgeons who say, "this is beyond my training."

After my last surgical doh-si-doh they sent me home advising me not to push too hard when I poop. And they were right, there are always consequences (I know, *TMI*).

I think a lot about my dura mater. About it's functions and layers and tissue strands. I like to imagine it bluish and thrumming and whole.

I like to imagine it un-impinged and glistening. If only wishful thinking could heal. I know some people think that prayer will save me, and while I am open to any possibility I have never been persuaded by religion. I am more of the stoic sort who muddles through. At least this is what I hope for myself, to be able to muddle through.

Muddling is not a very high bar, some would say. And maybe this is why people back away when I offer the truth of my predicament. Because I am not looking to be the hero of my story. I am not doing battle and I am certainly not hoping to overcome my disability. Instead I'm aiming towards adapting to the moving target of my mobility sweet spot, the strange algebraic equation that adds up to the sum of getting anything done: priority of task divided by how many minutes I can be on my feet multiplied by the current severity of compression on my spinal cord (at multiple levels) equals are we done yet? Welcome to zero.

I have written before about the dance of possibility and the elegance of letting go. I have thrown most of it in the trash. Because, what is the point? What is gained from talking about this or from revealing the inner workings of how a person makes sense of this kind of unwanted personal change? I have written and discarded and written again. Because I struggle with how angry it makes me to have to explain being disabled in an ableist culture. Because I remember what it felt like when my body worked better and I ache for a long walk on the beach. Because aging will be full of physical complexity for me and I already get pissed off at people who can walk. And I don't want to feel what I feel about all of this, let alone have it served up for brunch in the day-by-day cafe.

Dura mater, the tough mother. What has she still got to teach me now that I have learned the trick of how to dance only in my mind? My hope for getting through all this as gently as possible is not a poet's delicate 'thing with feathers'. My hope is a rumbling shamanic chant that resonates in my core, a wildness that glistens and thrums with life and neural impulse. Que sera sera.

To Each Her Own:

I am 58 years old and, proudly, I have never shaved my armpits. Never. Not once. I always considered it a barbaric assault on tender skin. My mother shaved, or didn't, depending on her whim. Almost all of my friends did and still do. My daughters go back and forth according to their moods and say that to them shaving is unimportant either way.

I have hairy legs too, which people tend to notice more often than my underarms. The boys in fourth grade (and seventh, and still in twelfth) were terribly rude about it. I endured their derision and tried to ignore it. Nobody was especially concerned with calling out sexist bullies back then. I am pretty sure there were guys who chose not to date me because of my choice to keep my body hair intact. I always considered myself lucky not to have to get to know them better.

My grandmother warned that if I wore a skirt to a job interview I would never get hired. To her my hairy legs were a telling comment on my personal hygiene, which she acknowledged was otherwise acceptable. For a few years the only time my legs encountered a razor was before a visit with her. This way we could skip the whole topic, along with any conjecture about my sexuality (since, as every one knew back then, lesbians don't shave their legs "so it must be a sign," her sister whispered in the kitchen). I have not shaved my legs since my Gram died in 1992.

I have never plucked an eyebrow either.

I have sensitive skin, prone to rashes and irritation. Why bring more misery on myself with razor blades? Honestly, my hairy legs glide more smoothly across the sheets without stubble. And yes, the man I married couldn't care less whether or not I shave. In the thirty some-odd years we have co-habited, he has never worn a tie and I have never shaved my body hair. (Except for semi-annual visits to grandma and that one time when curiosity got the best of us and he helped me shave "down there". Of course I got a terrible rash.)

Clearly I am not ruled by vanity when it comes to body hair. Well... most body hair. I got older. Raised children. Acquired crow's feet, brow furrows, and chin hairs.

The chin hairs challenge my equanimity. There were just a few here and there at first. Then I noticed my heretofore ignored mustache became more pronounced, sprouting the odd wisp. I would pluck at the chin when I couldn't stand it any more. I applied heated wax to the upper lip, tearing it away with cloth strips. And of course, I got a rash. My hair removal systems were inefficient and finally one morning, staring at myself in the mirror with all the lights turned up bright, it seemed like the only solution was to shave. With a man razor. My chin. My upper lip. Just now and then, I promised myself. I'll never have a five o'clock shadow, right?

Nowadays, I shave on average four times a week. I hate the stubble and the way it scrapes my husband's face when I kiss him good morning. I love the smooth that follows in the razor's wake. I make fun of myself in the mirror for being vain. I have learned to buy better quality razors and to moisturize well.

There is a patch of black hair, three quarters of an inch or so across, that sprouts slightly left of center about halfway down my double chin. I can't help but see that some people are distracted by that patch of hair and I try to forgive them for what they can't help. For years I did not shave away that most noticeable flaw. I left that patch of hair alone because it poked at my vanity, reminding me of why I bother to shave any where at all. Finally though, it started to bother me and on special occasions I'd shave it away, until finally every time I shave is a special occasion and I am less bothered by neck stubble than I was by a patch of neck fur.

Most importantly, I have come to accept this vain woman who looks back at me in the mirror. The hair on my face grew in just as predictably as the hair in my armpits did. Like the body hair that signals puberty, these changes are a sign of maturing naturally and of deepening womanhood. As I shave hair away I am aware that I am trying to erase some part of myself in order to appear more in sync, or at least less out of touch, with the norms of feminine beauty. It is a compromise I make over and over again. Because... vanity. It's forgivable.

Recently, the mirror shows me new rogue hairs sprouting at enthusiastic angles from my eyebrows. My grandma had these too; she plucked hers. I am keeping mine in place. To each her own.

Zero over Pi

Not every day you come up hard, face to face with the harm resulting from a complicated childhood. Except it is every day that you contend with it. And when you do come face to face, and all the wishing it had been different slides away, what matters are the words you can say about yourself that are true. And to tell the truth, that word 'harm' is a wicked tricky one for me.

The myth in the family I grew up in was that, despite evidence otherwise, we were not harmed by our parents' narcissism and benign neglect. My brother left home at 16, I got out the door at 15. We hit the road and hitchhiked off with our parents blessings and invitation to return. Years later we compared notes and realized that despite both of us trying at one point or another, there was never a way to come home. It wasn't until I was living with my own teenage children and truly understood the care and feeding of an adolescent person that it occurred to me; no one would leave home at that age if home felt safe.

Not too long ago I experienced an epiphany at my mother's dining room table that caused me to get up and leave her house. Not so much angry as just done (for the moment). We get along well most of the time and genuinely appreciate the friendship we have grown into. I don't want to work it out, there is nothing to fix. The next time we see each other it will all, genuinely, be well enough. Because this late in the game the better choice is to let it go. The epiphany, the treasure in the heart of the sorrow, is mine to keep and it comes with understanding and healing that will do me a life time of good. I drove off with one hand over my heart, my face wet with tears, saying over and over to myself, "I am willing to believe I am lovable."

Because there is not much in my childhood that confirmed this, and over lunch my mother reminded me of my flaws in the most benign yet twisted way (her 'em oh', uh oh!); I talk too loud, I'm bossy, too sensitive, whatever. I had to leave the house to be able to give myself a different message. Just like I left home at 15 to give myself another life. I am willing to believe I am lovable.

When I was 17, supporting myself with house cleaning and babysitting jobs, a woman I worked for gently helped me off a step stool and sat me in front of a mirror. Somehow she recognized that I had never been shown how to preen. She whispered a blessing and reached in to teach me, making me giggle as we experimented with little changes to help myself feel pretty. I still think of her when I do that one thing with my hair to be fancy.

Every now and then a door in the memory palace opens on a moment in my life when I was appreciated and encouraged just for being. The door opens to memories of times people asked the right question, recognized my need to be better supported, and leaned in. The babysitter who taught me how to make my own breakfast, the outsider aunt, the junior high school art teacher who gave me sanctuary and chores in her classroom. Its as if all of them whispered into my ear a blessing for my future that is still doing me some good.

I worry some about the ways my children (and my brother's) have inherited the consequences of this harm to our own

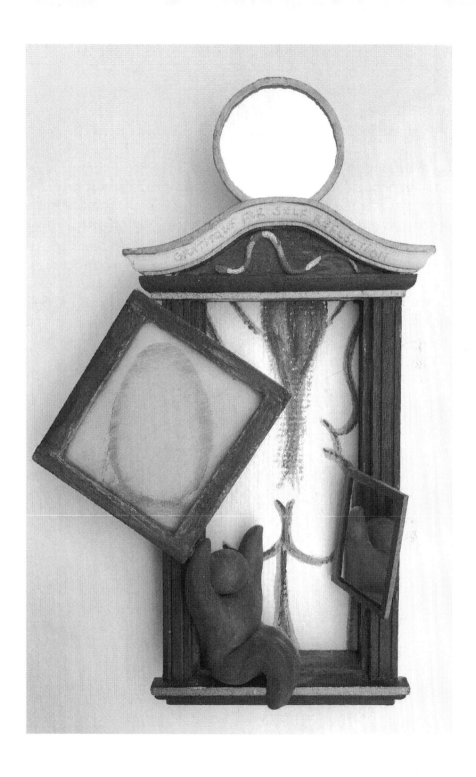

child-selves. If I could I would spare them all of this. My brother and I both recognize the flotsam and jetsam left in the wake of having to try so very hard to believe in ourselves and to belong. Our kids, certainly, are not immune to the burdens of this hereditary luggage.

I am not always ok, although I try hard to look like I am. I often expect to fail, surprised when I am wrong and it turns out right. It's a delicate balance, having the chutzpah to exist at all. Some mornings I wake up curled around the tender animal-child self within whispering blessings of encouragement that I hope I will hear across the whole arc of my time, that I breathe in deep to take to heart. It is ok to be beautiful. My success does not take away from someone else. I am lovable. L'chaim.

For some time, while emptying the e-mail trash, I snipped and collected odd lines of grammatically intriguing sex related spam-speak. The pile of phrases grew, expanded, and organized into something more interesting, which I offer now for your entertainment:

Hung Like a Horse

Forget about foreclosures, unemployment and recession! Enough downsizing, I'm ready to outsize! It's time for a new diversion, maybe even a lifestyle change. The daily onslaught of enthusiastic e-testimony that I delete has inspired me to consider the benefit of acquiring manly attributes of my own. Yup, it's my penis I want to talk about here, and judging from the steady stream of spam arriving in my e-mail junk-box, the status of my stick is causing quite a stir.

One after another, expansive correspondents invite me to free my 'artful willy'. I am certain they are meaning to address someone else because, truth be told, I may be artful but I haven't got a willy. Nor do I posses a molten rod, love wand, or sword of delight with which to pleasure the hordes of horny women hungry for hard humping. But apparently I can fix all that.

Each week, hundreds of people from all over the world express concern for the circumference, length and tumescence of my potential potence. As the hidden properties of my latent love tool are laid out, I have a swelling desire to correct the inadequacies of my penis. Now I imagine growing one myself! If predictions are correct, I can't wait to show my friends! My trouser mouse will soon become a monster schlong. I'll never be bored again!

If these claims are to be believed then it's time to upgrade my sex tool. I've been promised that I can increase my love stick to make it really magic because, judging from new evidence, a rock hard boner is not unachievable! Just this morning I was offered an exclusive penis increasing preparation that will help me gain the greatest custard launcher ever!

Scientists have just discovered an elixir which guarantees that rooster-challenged persons can improve their lot with super size and vigor for their love weapon! In case I retain a shred of skepticism or my libidinous curiosity remains to be satisfied, I have been barraged with 'true confessions of real women' (what, as opposed to inflatable?) who finally and conclusively acknowledge that big phalli are more attractive! And once I've memorized the ten hottest things to say to a woman in bed I will be proud that my yogurt-gun is getting so much action.

The person who wrote to assure me that all hotties love a big thumper really straightened me out; why hold back? Since the insufficient size of my male package can now be changed, I'm sure the additional inches will make me a champion in bed. I am even beginning to believe that my love sausage will win more prizes; why, I've been promised that my all natural mega-size wang doodle will make my lover sigh with desire! Expert sources assure me that friends will admire my new man-part and when I allow my rod to elongate until it is a male feature truly worthy of Casanova, I'm going to love the way you look at it.

Polls show that my life will be better lubricated once I believe that my beef-whistle can really grow beyond it's present size. I'm almost tempted to find out if any of these preparations, pills and mechanical devices will have an improbable effect on my phallus, making it bigger and more solid; but am I really ready to hear every one scream my name in passion when they see the improved strength of my purple-helmeted warrior of love?

Someone went so far as to send a link to pictures with this message, in fact, this is the e-mail that finally swayed me.

I live out in the woods, and without a high speed internet connection I couldn't see the images but I sure got the picture: it read, "This is your thingy. And this is your thingy on meds. Any questions?" Well, I do have a question. In my mind's eye I can see it's a willy, but is it artful yet?

My ten year old daughter asked the other day, "Mom, what's a boner?" The answer on the tip of my tongue was, "It's a male feature worthy of Casanova!" But I caught myself, realizing I would have to explain who Casanova was and what he needed a bone for. Instead, I told her it was another word for penis that people sometimes use when talking about sex. This was already more than she wanted to know. Thank goodness she doesn't read her spam!

With such a variety of exciting offers to choose from, I confess that it is infinitely entertaining to imagine what it would be like to go through life differently equipped. But enough exhilaration, I'm delighted with my own anatomy. For those of you born with a groin ferret, beware! If you read your spam, the inchworm in your pants might some day be hung like a horse of a different color. Carpe pipinnae!

Chag Sameach Bubeleh

When I was a second grader I carried a menorah to school for show and tell. I lived in a rural Connecticut town, far enough from New York City that there were only five Jewish kids in the entire elementary school. I was so excited to share with my classmates the story of the Macabees celebrating in the ruins of the temple and the miracle of the oil that burned for eight days. To tell them about dreidel games, latkes, jelly donuts; singing and lighting candles.

Like every American kid with a television set, Charlie Brown and his gang had taught me the true meaning of Christmas and I knew all about Rudolf, Santa, and the Abominable Snow Man. I learned Christmas carols at school and even my Beys Yaakov educated mother knew the words to Silent Night. Without considering that assimilation is never a two way street or thinking there might be consequences, I stood in front of the class and held up my family's menorah. It was a little unwieldy for my seven year old hand and I remember noticing the colored wax on it from the candles we burned the night before.

All of a sudden a classmate stood up in the back of the room, pointed right at me, and started screaming at the top of her lungs. I stared hard at her knees jutting out from under the lacy hem of her dress because I was afraid to look at her face. It is the first reference I heard of the Holy Ghost, who was called upon to strike me down because the Jews, and I, had killed Jesus.

I could not have been less prepared for this, and our teacher clearly wasn't prepared either because she sent me out into the hall where I sat alone in my coat-cubby, hugging the menorah to my trembling chest and trying not to hear the hoof beats of Cossacks (always so near in the imagination of a Jewish kid whose Bubbe tells stories of hiding). I have no idea what the teacher said to my classmates. I was eventually fetched from the hall during a penmanship lesson and no one looked up from their paper as I slid into my seat. At recess the boys stuffed rocks into snow balls and pelted me, calling names and joking about ovens. Seriously, children taunting about ovens, Connecticut circa 1969.

I got off the school bus angry that day. Why had my mother let me take the menorah to school? Should someone have warned me that a story about olive oil could provoke a hysterical classmate into accusing me of being personally responsible for killing her God? Was this why my father ranted against any religion? I can't remember now what happened after I got into the kitchen and found my mother's arms.

What I do remember is lighting the menorah that evening at sundown in the front window of a modest house on a country road; five little lights shining into the night. Feeling bruised still from my day at school I asked my mother if we could light the candles in a back window instead. She said no, it wouldn't do to hide. "We put our light where a passer-by can see, so that any wandering Jew will know they're welcome at our table." We sang Sevivon and Moaz Tzur, and then 'This Little Light of Mine' with a touch of irony even a seven year old could appreciate as we sat watching the candles drip wax on the windowsill until they had sputtered out.

That night at bedtime my mother taught me Yiddish phrases so I could vex the schoolyard bullies (may your nose grow like an elephant's trunk to blow up your ass/an elafants sh-tam aroyf deyn tokhes), the translations providing the good medicine of laughter, though neither of us thought for a moment that the events of my day were funny. "Chag Sameach, bubeleh," my mother said, tenderly kissing me good night.

I raised my own kids in a rural town in New England where they, too, were among a small handful of Jews in their school. The youngest one had her own 'Jews killed Jesus' Christmas season moments with a misguided classmate who followed and taunted her at recess. I told my kid that if he didn't stop she should punch him. And then I went to check in with the school principal, just in case my kid hauled off and hit someone (even though she knew it's always better to use her words) and then told the grown ups "my mom said I could". I told him I didn't want to make a scene about anti semitism on the play ground. Our principal was a transplanted Jewish kid from the Bronx, not a native New Englander. He had mastered the face of professional neutrality; neither of us spoke for a long minute. Then he looked me right in the eye as if I had not just told him I gave my kid permission to punch someone, as if all the fight in me was ok with him. And because he and I both know that on Hanukah we celebrate some bad ass Macabees, he told me he'd talk to the other kids parents that evening and make it stop, and then he said, gently, "Chag Sameach bubeleh, Chag Sameach."

On Re-writing My Father's Obituary

As I attended the bedside of my dying father, his wife
brought me a box of family memorabilia to sort. Her delivery was unceremonious, even curt. I tried to believe it wasn't
hostile but she said, "May as well take home what you want
of this," then turned away, without saying out loud 'don't let
the door hit your ass on the way out'.

Which is what my dad had just said to me, "I'm on my way
out, sweet heart." He took my face in his hands, kissed both
cheeks and my forehead then held my head tight to his chest,
squeezing me into his failing heart. He named the people we
held in common, my brother and the grandchildren, my husband, my mother. And then it was time for me to go. I carried
the box with photos of his parents out to the car, fumbled
with my seat belt and drove off stunned. I was hours down
the highway when the call came that he was gone. Twenty
minutes later I had to pull over and throw up. It felt like I'd
been sucker punched. Empty, I wiped my face, overcome
by a strange afterglow of mirth tinged with irony. I drove
off again feeling untethered and muttering at the oncoming
headlights, "So, this is how it goes when my father dies."

In a few days his wife emailed the obituary she'd written and
had published. I could feel his ghostly wincing as I read it.
It's not that it lied, rather that it leaned. Parts of his life had
been romanticized and others erased. So, using the bits that
I thought he'd want kept, I wrote another obituary around
it and had it published in my home town paper. I left in the
truth that his second wife had been the love of his life, and I
left their story as she told it. The rest, the part about my family of origin and about the man who raised me, I restored.
Radically, with my fist raised in defiance, just how a man
with some revolutionary bona fides would wish to be remem-
bered.

What many people want when they have lost a parent is reassurance that they have been a good child, a loved child, a loving child; or good enough and loving enough. It is the rare person who is confident they have been loved enough.

From the day he died, my father's wife never let me back into their house. I'd gotten pulled into a falling out she'd had months before over an ugly exchange of words with my brother which resulted in the heartbreak of my father and brother not speaking in the last months of his life, until a week before he died. Because it matters (so much) who we are when faced with death's necessity, my dad and brother came to peace on their last visit; easily, wordlessly, with all the aching love needed to repair what could be repaired. But we are still shunned by his widow. Some years later, while visiting my father's oldest friends I discovered that she'd spoken ill of me to them. I wish this didn't rankle, but it does.

Seriously, look up the list of synonyms for the word rankle, I have been in all of those states of being over this relational chasm. I keep hoping I can stop giving a hoot. Here's the bit that stings: I would have liked to rest in my dad's chair at the table one last time to savor his view of the bay. I would have adopted little things from his toolboxes and desk that I know he'd been keeping for more than 60 years, through all his moves, marriages, and reinventions. I would have treasured the small random sewing machine parts from his fathers repair shop in the Bronx and other bits of flotsam that are jettisoned after a death. I would like to have more than memories, a box of photos, and sparse family records; something small to keep in my pocket and be reminded of him on days when being loved enough would do me some good.

I made an attempt at tidying recently and came across three creased issues of the local newspaper that my version of dad's obituary was published in. I'm still proud of myself. The act of writing the obit and of resisting a twisted history, even if it means being unforgiven, goes a long way towards balancing the rankle in how I remember my father. And in how I am comforted by remembering him. I'm not confident I was loved enough. I am confident I was loved, and this is the blessing of enough.

As read from the stage of the Great Falls Word Festival at the Shea Theater, in Turners Falls, MA in October, 2018, just days after the fatal shootings at the Tree of Life shul in Pittsburgh

An Elefant's Shtam

This is a story about a gust of wind. It is a story about disappointment. And it is not the story I rehearsed to tell tonight, so please forgive that I need to have pages to keep me on track.

During WWII, Jews in Budapest were brought to the edge of the Danube, ordered to remove their shoes, and shot dead, falling into the river below. This is the very short version of how my grandmother's shoes were not left on the bank of the Danube river.

In 1921 a neighbor brought my family warning just minutes before soldiers crashed through their front gate looking for Jews to harm. When a soldier climbed the ladder to the attic where they hid, my grandfather (a pious Rabbi) held aside his beard to contribute a breath. He blew out the candle and decades later in a kitchen in Brooklyn I was told the soldier, who must have been afraid of the dark, went away muttering about a squirrel. My grandparents, their children, and the neighbor who warned them all, lived. And the breath that snuffed out the soldiers candle brought a voice to my grandfather's ear that he took as instruction from an angel of God. He left for America a few months later and within two years my grandmother sailed from Hamburg on a ship named The Majestic, in steerage for a week with six children, in order to join him.

You get the point. We are survivors. We turn ourselves towards life.

This is not the story I planned to tell you tonight, but after the shooting at the Tree of Life shul in Pittsburgh it is the one my DNA commands I tell.

Many years after my grandmother told me the story of the soldier and the candle and the breath of destiny in the attic, I discovered that my grandfather had written a traditional death bed document, a viyduy, apologizing to my grandmother for bringing her to America, a place which deeply disappointed him because the cultural atmosphere was morally unclean for an observant Jewish family. He lamented coming to this country and was sorry he could not live to return them all to Europe. He died in 1933, six years before the Nazi's drove their tanks into Poland. If he had lived he would have thanked the angel that whispered in his ear to emigrate. Almost all the family who stayed behind were lost in the war, we say lost, but really they stepped out of their shoes and were shot on the bank of the Danube River, or sent off on trains to die by Nazi design.

All sorts of people have a story like my family's, a story of events so terrible it would cause them to leave behind home, family, livelihood, even the graves of their ancestors. No matter the risks or hugeness of the unknown. No matter the possibility of disappointment. Despite the Rabbi's death bed regret there are now over a thousand descendants who name my Hungarian grandparents as their own. I don't know how to end this story, because we are still being hunted and harmed. From my other grandfather, who was not a Rabbi and had no patience for anti semites, I inherited the story of the time he knocked a guy out cold for calling him a 'kike' when he was buying wine for Passover. Following his example I have taught my otherwise peaceful children that it is ok to punch Nazis. And I taught them the same Yiddish curse my mother taught me to throw back at bullies in the streets: an elafants shtam aroyf deyn tokhes (may your nose grow like an elephant's trunk to blow up your ass). Always a good idea to balance temper with humor. These are unbearable and dark times. The safety we have grown comfortable with has been so easily shattered.

Please, do this thing with me: put your hand over your heart and listen through your fingers to the beat of your own life thrumming through this muscle which is the size of your fist. Take a breath with me. And another breath. Wiggle your toes. Thank the ancestors for the courage they have passed on to us. Yes, you feel it too. You get the point, we are survivors, we turn ourselves towards life. L'chaim.

cups of sorrow thrown into the ocean
(with a tip o' the pen to Wislawa Szymborska's poem
'Consolation')

I went to the beach yesterday to gather stones to give away at a funeral service. I live inland and it is a long drive, an effort, a labor of love. At the point in the road where the sky changes I opened the window to breathe in the salt air, my whole body excited by the change in atmosphere.

I went to the beach yesterday and sat at the bottom of the stairs that bring you from the top of the dune to the sandy shoreline. I sat with my hands in my lap, weeping, hoping no one walking by would notice the sloppy ragged tears. Digging my toes into the sand like a four year old, bereft and heartbroken. The seagulls stared and kept their distance. The waves continued to curl gently to shore. Finally the sorrow was spent and I could go searching for stones.

I went to the beach yesterday and found the long-dead flesh-less carcass of a giant sea turtle that gave me two bones. Later I found a cache of ancient whelk shells wedged by a recent storm into nooks and crannies in the breakwater, one of them hardly damaged and bigger than my hand. A tennis ball waited in the dry seaweed at the high tide line, a tease for the next dog to come along and give it purpose. And a matchbox race car sat stalled in the sand. There was a delicate feather with unusual black and white markings, I put it carefully in a pocket but when I looked later it had flown off again.

The stones that came to hand have edges and imperfections. Some of them shimmer. Even the small ones have a way of sitting in your palm or between your fingers with gravitas. This is how I choose them, the ones that have a weight that feels right in my hand are the ones given a place in my pockets. I am particular, many are touched and left. My vest gets damp, the pockets bulging and lumpy by the time I limp back towards the car.

I use my cane at the beach to help me along, to poke at things that I may not want to touch, leaning hard to bend and rise again when I find something interesting. I leave a trail of tripod tracks in the sand, two bare feet and a peg hole from the cane. A skilled tracker would tell you this person is foraging, is lame, and won't get far without resting. I sit again at the bottom of the stairs to watch the sea, and the day, and for the comfort of wiggling my toes some more in the sand. I am done throwing cups of sorrow into the ocean, reassured by the sea gifts, shell and bone and stone. Slightly mended. Ready to turn towards home again.

True Untrue

This is a story about radical kinship and Divine. It's an old story. And story is how we stay glued to the earth and to one another, the web we connect to our self with across the arc of our time. And no story is the same twice told because of that element, true untrue/untrue true, which side of the coin, whose version of how it all went down.

My story is I left home when I was 15 with a one way bus ticket from Springfield, Massachusetts to Albequerque, New Mexico, fifty dollars, and a letter from my father that had my picture with a notary's seal across it for proof, to whom it may concern, that I was not a runaway who needed to be returned. The plan was for me to hitch hike to the Rainbow Gathering near Truth or Consequences and then meander out to California and east again in a month's time. I'm still not sure how long my dad thought 50 bucks would feed me for on the road. I learned to improvise. This story is about the end of that trip and the long road home from Santa Cruz to Hadley, a five day odyssey that is so faded at the edges now that I only remember the highlight reel.

The Perseid Meteor shower made a spectacular show east of Salt Lake City high up in the Wasatch where Interstate 80 cuts through to the plains. From there I caught a ride from a woman with long blond hair in a converted Chevy yellow cab (painted sky blue) all the way to Cheyenne and then, one of the most interesting rides I ever had, from Cheyenne, Wyoming to Des Moines, Iowa in an RV with two leather vested bikers, a somewhat astounded twenty-something on walkabout, a teenage hippie chick (me), and a drag queen. The summer of 1977.

This strange cast of characters converged towards evening at a truck stop in Cheyenne, which in July of 1977 was not the shopping mall and hipster metropolis I imagine it has become today. It was a dusty dry crossroad in a world that was still cowboys and analog. Cheyenne was as redneck as could be and the two bikers, the walkabout, the hippie chick, and the drag queen, well, none of our freak flags could really fold away so we found each other in the parking lot and quickly agreed it was safest to leave together.

We put one motorcycle inside the RV, strapped the other to the front bumper and then we all piled on board the Winnebago chariot and headed east towards Nebraska. Nebraska is long. We were all pretty stoned. The drag queen was headed to Chicago and needed company to stay awake and do drugs with. At some point in the wee hours our driver pulled over on the side of the highway and said "time to sleep".

I took my pack and sleeping bag outside so I wouldn't have to sleep with all those men and Walkabout came with me because it wasn't clear he felt entirely safe alone with the bikers or the drag queen. We slept for a few hours and sometime around 7am I woke up to flashing blue lights because a state trooper with that classic state trooper hat and swagger had pulled over to see what this RV was doing at the side of the road. With a motorcycle strapped to the front end. And a hippie chick waking up in the grass, and an oddly dressed man wearing lipstick and a nylon wig liner arriving in the doorway with a cigarette in a holder and a hand on his hip. The anti-trooper.

The Police asked for every one to come out where he could see us so the bikers rolled off the RV in their leather vests and biker boots and were not what he had been expecting at all, You could see he was thinking about possibly being outnumbered. Then he was leaning hard into the front seats to see what we had going on but was distracted by Walkabout who was up now and packing. The officer's attention swayed from his initial poking around the RV's front console. He came over to where I also had a bedroll on the ground.

A girl, not a woman. He looked me up. He looked me down. His uniform was crisp. He wanted to know how old I was, where I was coming from, where I was going, and who I was with. I'm on my own I told him, just met this crew yesterday. I handed him the unusual notarized letter from my dad. He asked me to unpack.

I grinned. Why certainly. I had books, pens, scarves, extra shoes, clothes, a rain poncho and here in the pockets I had herbs for natural healing. He was not much interested in the red hibiscus and goldenseal but the pennyroyal caught his eye and he got his nose in deep, looked at me and said, "is this marijuana?"

"Oh no," I told him, "that's pennyroyal and it helps women to keep their periods on time." Reaching for a bag of red raspberry leaf I said, "this is for menstruation too."

He handed the pennyroyal back fast, stuck his head in the side door of the RV, saw the other motorcycle and the rack of sequined evening gowns and decided that there would be too much paperwork. He warned us not to sleep on the side of the interstate and left, trusting us to pack up and go.

He had missed the bag of weed on the dashboard and the coke and spoon in the cup holder, and we hadn't gotten around to the peyote in my medicine bag. The mystery of menstruation is so powerful, and the taboo against men touching anything that has to do with lady-blood is so universal, that none of the men I was with were surprised the trooper had changed his mind about seeing everything in my bags. Our queer driver howled with laughter as we pulled back onto the interstate, the bikers said something grateful about witch magic, Walkabout decided the bikers and the drag queen were less scary than a 15 year old hippie chick. We parted ways at another truck stop in Des Moines, where I stayed on I-80 and the RV cut north to Chicago, where the drag queen had booked a two week run before heading back to Baltimore.

Yeah (quite possibly but not certainly) that Divine. Years later I caught up with John Waters' movies and my jaw dropped. Maybe, a teenage hippie chick's pennyroyal and the magic of menstruation kept two bikers, a walkabout, and a famous drag queen out of a Nebraska jail. And we all got to see Hairspray.

I made it home to the east coast with two more rides. One from Des Moines to Hartford in a semi hauling lettuce from Salinas to Boston. The next in a tiny MG from Hartford north along the river to Hadley, passing a fat joint with the Grateful Dead turned up loud. I rolled off I-91 at the Coolidge Bridge where I stood leaning over the railing to watch my tears float down into the Connecticut River. It was the moment I learned you don't really get to come home again because the girl who left no longer exists. It was the moment I understood that all the stories are true, and none of the stories are true, that our stories connect us to ourself across the arc of our time. It was the moment I began to know that true or untrue, its all just water under the bridge.

Solstice

The shortest day of a painful year and a long night to follow. As the sun climbs I struggle to hitch my spirits to it's ascent. I am not easily lifted in these times. I yearn for the unceasing fire of the sun to teach me to be fierce enough to turn my face towards the darkness ahead. I do not understand why human beings design systems of cruelty to impose on other human beings. But I also recognize in myself a callousness towards nature and life that causes me to turn away from people I know are in need, or to be wasteful of resources I understand are finite. It is an impulse, on the most personal level, to not see or correct actions, even though they cause harm. We cannot all be responsible for every thing, I tell myself, but is that collectively true? I am not innocent, therefore I must shoulder the responsibility to see the darkness in my world, in myself, and make corrections. Can I possibly be fierce and loving enough for this work? I don't have the hook of a faith tradition to hang my moral hat on, or a God to be protected or absolved by. What I have learned from others who have struggled and suffered for a just world is that we can be sustained by the smallest beauty: a weed blooming in the bleakest landscape, the kind smile of a stranger, the first bird that sings to the morning. In the light of this shortest day, I dare to face the darkness and to be sustained by the beauty yet to come.

(with a tip o' the pen to Dr. Maya Angelou)

102

Small Mercy

I got to play a part in a quasi-resurrection this afternoon. I was watching birds tussle at the feeder when a
chickadee collided with the window. It thumped and
fell face first into the snow on the deck; a small fragile
body with one wing askew. I held my breath, waiting
for it to pull it's head from the snow. It set it's wing
right first and then did a fancy little shimmy to adjust
it's tail. I expected again to see it's head come free.

The bird went still. I thought perhaps it had died. I
opened the glass door onto the deck and reached a
tentative hand, tugging gently at poised tail feathers,
then pulled away as the masked head popped out of the
snow with a curious cartoon grace. I ducked back inside
and shut the door.

The bird did not move. I thought I saw it's eye flicker
but I didn't have a straight view of it's face. I worried
that if I moved closer, or fast, it would panic. Then it's
beak came up a fraction as if it was sniffing for equilibrium, the head tilting ever so slightly to bring an ear out
of the wind. It was collecting itself. Maybe if I gave it
some privacy it could get launched again.

Retreating to work I found myself thinking about February. It does have a way of smacking you in the head
and leaving you stunned for a bit. February is never
subtle for me. I get dazzled by the thaw and then reality
sets in with mud, slush, and too much light reflecting
off the snow in the blinding slant of late afternoon sun.
I sometimes think it would help to have enough money
to fly myself off someplace warm. But I suspect I'd be
disoriented any place this time of year.

I have been working in my studio on a collage that uses
a shed snake skin to communicate my thoughts about

GRATITUDE FOR INCARNATION

transformation, but 'transformation' is too neat a package for what I want to convey. There is this little nuance to it, a twist I want to make in the perspective of the piece that sets it more rightly in the spiritual physics of what we shed and leave on the floor when we've grown out of our skin; that fine dry outer layer that is the boundary between inside and out. An almost transparent, patterned, and perfectly textured relic which nevertheless suggests forward or outward momentum.

It is easier for me to bend words around this concept than it is to use skin, paint, glue, wood, glass and something vaguely pearlescent as a vessel to contain and express the layers of this particular riff. Still, the words seem ungainly on the page, close but no cigar (which is another February riff). I think again of the chickadee, adjusting wing and tail with it's head still trapped in the snow, released, then tilting towards equilibrium and waiting. I walk back to look out onto the deck.

No bird. Just an impression in white and shadow that says wing, tail, and perching toe. Where it's head had been stuck there's a hole in the snow just about the size of a birdhouse opening. The whole of it evokes an image of having been here and being elsewhere in the blink of an eye. A feathered absence glittering in the afternoon sun. Like the snake that shed it's skin where I could find it, the bird has left layers of identity echoing in what remains.

Later in the afternoon I bring my six year old daughter to the window and tell her the bird tale. Mostly it is the echo of bird she sees in the snow but she believes that I saved it. Her belief is a small mercy, another quasi-resurrection. This time of a different small feathered thing: my perching hope for equilibrium, and deepest gratitude for being understood even though it's February and I keep smacking my head on tilting existential boundaries.

Housewife Blues

In 2013, at the age of 56, my husband was laid off from the non profit educational tech firm he had co-founded eighteen years before. His founding partner had retired and the new company president decided to "re-brand". It was painful then, it is still painful now. The day he came home with the dismissal letter I was standing on the deck watching a spectacular Spring sunset fade into evening. Our middle daughter was about to graduate high school. He came up the steps silently and handed me the letter. I read half way down the page, looked up at him, made sure I had solid eye contact and said, "I'm with you."

It is a moment I have thought about often since. In the first months, when I was acutely concerned with how he was feeling I was just relieved I hadn't said something more along the lines of "Oh fuck!" Then, as the months of his unemployment lengthened into half a decade and our thirty five years of shared savings dwindled literally to nothing, "I'm with you" has gained substance.

Here's the thing. I know we are not alone, I know that other formerly middle class people are also not quite making ends meet. Or they're taking third jobs to stay afloat. Or selling off a car and making due with one between three drivers. I know that other parents haven't been able to afford to send their kids to college, or camp, or pay for music lessons, or even public school athletic fees. I know that not every one can afford to make the holidays happy this year, let alone swing a Valentine's surprise. I know we are not alone and that there is a lot of invisible pain rolling with us here in the deep, where the American Dream is in trouble.

I am college educated and, with three kids, for much of our marriage I was a stay at home mom with side gigs like driving a school bus. I've earned three graduate level professional certificates over the last five years, hoping to translate a small portion of our savings into making myself more employable.

For a while I went back to social work, but I brought home a little over $3/hour in take home pay, the rest of my check was eaten by the family's decent health insurance coverage. Which it turns out I needed for a series of spine surgeries which made the job a moot point. I tried to get state rehab services after the surgeries but could not because of our remaining savings; while my physical disabilities put me at 'priority 1', until we 'spent down' and hit rock-bottom financially there would be no help available.

When it got harder to pay the bills on time my husband rose from his professional self-exile, and bartered with a neighbor for a haircut. In exchange he gave her a few pounds of fresh shiitake mushrooms that he's been cultivating in the years he has not been traditionally employed. The haircut-shiitake barter was a beginning. Next he stopped into the thrift store on family discount day and bought new-to-him pants, shirt, and shoes so he'd feel more confident at an interview. He has lost a lot of weight and looks fly in the better fitting clothes. Then a lifelong friend took him along to a trade show where geeks who make gadgets mingle with nerds who have budgets. My husband came home somewhat restored, with a spark I had not seen in a long time. I'm with you, I thought to myself, trying not to hope too hard that his spark would rise to a flame. In the next weeks he sent resumes out. He said one person he spoke to asked if he'd relocate. "I'm with you," I told him.

So yeah, about that American Dream and our adjusted expectations, suffice it to say this is not how we anticipated approaching retirement age. I've been thinking lately about Mark Twain, whose personal financial ups and downs seem mostly not to have gotten the better of his pen or wit. I find myself wishing I too could set sail for the Continent in order to delay communications. It takes so much momentum to maintain equilibrium in the modern global digital economy, a little wobble can make your whole house of cards suddenly precarious.

Twain wrote, "It ain't what you don't know that gets you in trouble. Its what you know for sure that just ain't so." All along the way we could have made different choices. I know we have friends who wonder why I didn't "force" my husband to get work sooner. All the ancient housewife wisdom I could haul up from the bottom of the well indicated to me that reimagining his relationship with work had to rise from his own necessity, not mine.

A housewife's work is tending the needs and mending the sorrows of her family. Rides, paperwork, hot soup and biscuits. Because I needed some place fertile and beautiful to balance all of that, I leaked my own blues and eccentricities into my garden, where the hummingbirds and bumble bees come to dance. Over the years, because accidents happen, my family has expressed a talent for breaking my favorite kitchen things. Eventually all the cracked mugs and bowls and a variety of other injured knick knacks have found their way into my garden; I weave the broken things in with the beauty there. The garden is the place I go to tend and mend myself. Lately my husband has been building me new beds to plant in. It is his contribution to mending my housewife blues.

"I'm with you." Three short words. At the marriage altar we find the words to say 'I choose you' while wrapping them in finery and rainbows. No one tells you in the beginning that its not a one time deal, that you will have to keep on choosing. That this choosing is an ongoing acceptance of responsibility for more than you could ever imagine you were committing yourself to.

We both come from families that came apart before childhood had fully ripened us for life. We carry impairments from early trauma, we have soft spots like bruised fruit. This doesn't make us special, but it does make us a little quirky, and possibly more flexible when things go awry.

There was a moment we shared in the hospital room after a second spine surgery had not gone so well and we weren't sure whether I'd be able to sit upright again, ever, without blinding head pain. I lay flat on the hospital bed with my body tilted slightly on pillows so I could see my husband a few feet away where he sat very still in the chair provided.

Hospital furniture is somehow never actually comfortable. I could see he was tired, and enormously worried, and trying not to show either. We really wanted most of all to help each other laugh but it would be another day and a half before we were sure I could sit up and only then did we actually exhale. So we didn't say much during his visit and what I remember is the grace of an encouraging, constant and unspoken 'I'm with you' woven through-and-through in the silence between us.

With our savings depleted our three and half decade long marriage has crossed a boundary into a time of uncertainty. We will be changed by this, each of us stretched and folded to accommodate a life that has already been drastically reshaped by circumstance. In the best moments we spoon in the morning without saying much, or sit in the yard hold-ing hands; appreciating that our peace with one another is a thing that mostly has not changed. We'll dig out or tunnel through somehow and adjust the way we live to whatever ne-cessity throws our way. We'll make do, and we'll make each other laugh, and do our best not to know for sure so that what 'just ain't so' doesn't bite us in the ass.

My husband went off to job interviews with tech companies and much to everyone's relief had partial success. He was at least fifteen years older than every one else he worked with on the first project. He taught himself two new coding languages in less than three months while living all week in a city two hours from home. It worked in part because the friend he stayed with provided dogs to come back to at the end of the day. And because the city is the one he grew up in and he already knew how to survive there. I'd wake every weekday morning in a house on a dirt road in the woods, without him, and tell the dog about my dreams and troubles. My husband would text me a picture of something beautiful, like a flower encountered on his walk to the subway. I'd text him back a selfie of me and the dog. Here is what I learned again every morning sitting at the edge of the bed, choosing again the reservoir of good will that is this life; 'I'm with you' is the blessing of enough.

Already this story is old news. Already the next wave of hardship has come and we are treading water again. Doing the best we can. Finding ways to make each other laugh.

He saved a frog from the cat the other day and brought me to see where it was recovering in a flower pot in the garden of broken things. One of the kids got a new job and I've got a new side gig. In an odd way it is a relief to be spared the anxiety of having all our savings invested in the stock market, after spending down we're reduced to having just our wits to spin a new American Dream with. We have become old married people, with appreciations and peeves. In the morning we sit on the edge of the bed and lean in, a silent 'I'm with you'.

We are learning how to grow saffron now, the fragrant threads are the stigmas of a fall crocus that comes into bloom after the mushroom project has subsided. Better times call to us like voices that carry a long way across the water; we don't know yet if we'll find a way towards that shore. Meanwhile, I hum these housewife blues and putter in the garden of broken things. May it continue to provide solace and sustain us.

~

Dina Stander is the author of the poetry collection Old Bones & True Stories. She is an End-of-life Navigator, funeral celebrant, burial shroud maker, and founder of the Northeast Death Care Collaborative.

If you go to her website at www.dinastander.com please visit the page for the Phone of the Wind. A practitioner of radical kinship, Dina is grateful, always, for the creative community that helps her lamp shine steady and bright.

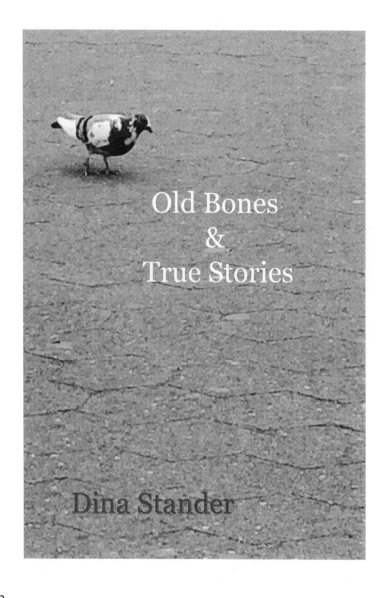

Made in the USA
Middletown, DE
23 November 2021

52726422R00068